Sex Pot

Sex Pot, the Marijuana Lover's Guide to Gettin' It On.

Copyright © 2011 Mamakind

Published by Quick American Publishing

A division of Quick Trading Company

Piedmont, CA

ISBN 13: 978-1-936807-00-0

Project Director: Jack Jennings
Project Manager: Angela Bacca
Editor: Angela Bacca
Cover and Interior Design: Hera Lee
Illustrations: Niko [excluding images on pp. 1-11]

Special thanks to SKUNK Magazine for assistance in this publication.

Printed in China

The material offered in this book is presented as information that should be available to the public. The Publisher does not advocate breaking the law. However, we urge readers to support the secure passage of fair marijuana legislation.

Try your bookstore first but you may order this book from our website—www.quicktrading.com

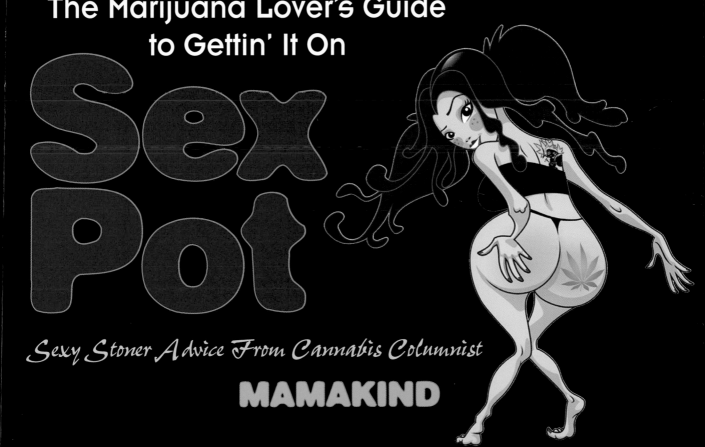

The Marijuana Lover's Guide to Gettin' It On

Sex Pot

Sexy Stoner Advice From Cannabis Columnist

MAMAKIND

To my husband and to everyone I've ever slept with and/or gotten high with. May all your buds and STDs be well cured, always.

Big thanks to my family, especially to my mom for both giving me a sense of humor and hope that a career slinging words is possible. I know she'll buy this book but hope she doesn't read it. To my husband, John, who has never questioned my ability to kick ass with a pen. I love you—stop laughing. Thanks to Marc Emery for setting me on this remarkable career path, showing me what anti-prohibitionism really means. Big, long hugs to Dana Larsen for his unconditional love. Double-kiss, naughty smirks and an ass slap for Marc-Boris St-Maurice. To MotherThirteen & J.R. for introducing me to the wonders of polyamory. To Rebecca, Sita, Puff Mama & Tracy for being my stonerchick heroes. Mandy my love, for going beyond the call of duty. To Jay, even though he thinks I'm a heat score. To Silly, Kelly & Gerry: for officially being my longest relationships. To all my Calgary buds, especially Nick & Jacquie and in particular Keith & Debbie Fagin. To Ed Rosenthal for having faith in my work. Big hugs to Angela Bacca, without whom this book really wouldn't have happened. We'll share a CannaCosmo yet, sister. Finally, special thanks to where my heart & soul resides, SKUNK Magazine. To Niko for his artistic genius (thanks for the skinny arms). Len, Kat, Soula, Attilio, The Rev, Chad and yes, you too Seth. Above all, I thank John Vergados, capriciousness and all. I owe you some fried eggs, man.

INSIDE

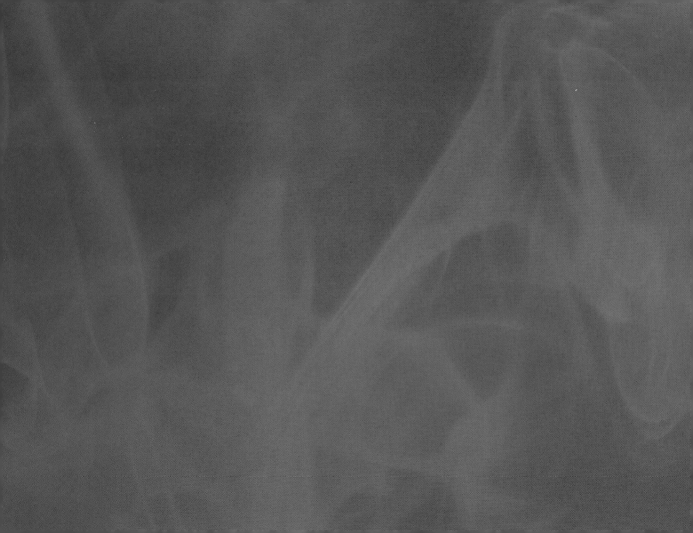

Introduction:
ROACHPLAY and OTHER NICETIES

I know some of you consider yourselves hard core tokers; otherwise, you wouldn't be reading this particular book. I'd bet my best Nepalese Temple and benwa balls that some of you are hard core sex monkeys, too. It's amazing how often these attributes go hand-in-hand…

So let's not talk about how you and Cindy Lou puffed a little grass and got kinda frisky when you were seventeen and made sweet, sweet love under a be-jeweled canopy of stars.

Let's talk about the spacecake-induced orgy you had at that house party. The jellyhash-assisted anal probing. The hookah-enabled masturbation.

Not just sex on drugs…sex with drugs. What happens when you plaster a tab of acid to her swollen clit with your tongue? When you slather her velvet valley with the finest of honey oils?

There will be no Prada in this sex column, nay; my size twelves won't allow it (put it away, ToeBoy). My qualifications lie in my commitment to gainful employment requiring blastedness and nudity, like a painter's model and *SKUNK Magazine* sex columnist.

I'm a bisexual, polyamorous, swinging Prairie BudBabe, ex-West Coast CheebaChick, former Montreal MarijuanaMaven, I am everything you are and some shit you ain't never heard of. Believe me, I encourage anything that contributes to the Total Being Orgasm, so if you have anything to share that you think might curl my hair, BRING IT ON.

Alternatively, if you have any burning questions regarding pleasures of the flesh, mind and spirit—and where the three shall meet—I'll do my darnedest to clear the smoke for you. If it requires a deep and personal investigation—oh yes, people, Mamakind cares to ease your cannabis/coital and psychedelic/sexual concerns that much.

All A Girl Wants

Well, since we're on the subject, boys and girls, let us explore the act that inspired the rant. How do y'all feel about the practice of "roachplay"?

Meaning: The skillful application of a hot cherry to one's skin by a partner or by yourself (depending on your kink) for the purpose of inducing a small amount of pain, which then can be transposed into an intense amount of pleasure.

When I've tried to bring it up with some lovers, I received the, "Gee, I could never do anything to hurt you, baby!" thing, much to my consternation.

Now, I've always respected my partners' boundaries, of course, but the sizzle of a glowing ember on my freshly licked nipple or clit does excite me so and needn't cause anything more than a fleeting dose of pain, if any!

Unless, in the heat of the hazy moment, the unpressed bubblehash chunga I was saving for post-coital relations is mistakenly grabbed for the utility doob. Then my bodacious tata is branded with molten trichomes and my hemp-cotton fuck towel is forever burned/stained in a vain attempt to quell what looks like Pele's Revenge on my breast. Do I ask too much?

A sensitive lover should have absolutely no problem sticking a hot knife

> I guess the entire world's a stage…mine just happens to have a big pole in the middle of it and a couple of plants under the lights.

up my ass if I ask him or her to. Right?

Okay, I'm hyperbolizing somewhat, but you get the point.

I guess the entire world's a stage… mine just happens to have a big pole in the middle of it and a couple of plants under the lights. Do remember, folks, that no matter what you're doing and/or with what, or whomever (you catch my drift). ALWAYS PLAY SAFE.

We all must do our part to make the world a better (and wetter) place, changing things one stoned skronk at a time. I love you all so very much. I wish I could line every last one of you up, human-bong you and give you oral pleasure!

Next to, "What's the best kinda weed, Mama?" (*heavy sigh*) the second most silly—uh, I mean poignant—question I'm asked is: "What's your favorite sexual encounter?" Well…there just isn't enough ink at the printers. So I'll give you the next best thing:

MAMAKIND'S TOP TEN GETTIN' IT ON SESSIONS. OH YEAH.

10 The first time. Okay, yeah, it was on the floor of some guy's room who my friends and I met just two weeks prior in the 7-Eleven. Yeah, he kept hitting me in the head with the rim of his baseball cap on the

A Bongslut is Born!

in-stroke, every time; yeah, he just turned the cap around when I said something instead of taking it off; yeah, I don't remember his name… something with a D…Darryl…Dennis…Dustin…but I do remember that it was so enjoyable that I came the first time and made him do it again. I salute you, Nameless Nova Scotian Boy Who (ironically) Worked at Red Lobster in Calgary, Alberta! When you laid me that night, you laid the first brick in my Foundation of Fuck.

9 Cumming while high. While it wasn't the first time I smoked pot or had a mind-blowing, self-induced orgasm, when I was 18 and got reeeeeeaally stoned on my birthday, toddled off to bed at approximately 4:20 a.m. and found out I couldn't get to sleep, I did what I always do—my fingers went to my SLEEP button. But this time, when I came, I almost touched the face of Krishna. A bongslut is born!

8 My first threesome. That I remember. Once again on my birthday (ain't I the lucky bitch?), my loving husband brought home the best present EVER: one of my best (male) friends. It was the gift that kept on cumming and yes, my friend still talks to me (I can't say as much for the husband).

7 Sex on psychedelics. Much like #9, I had done 'shrooms and had sex before. But when the two were put together—yeah. As long as you can keep from getting distracted by crazy things, like the floor. And don't puke (that's kind of a turn-off).

6 My first blowjob (that everybody had to hear about). What can I say? It was in the pool in my apartment building. It became apparent at a fairly tender age that yo Mama is a skilled fellatist. It also became apparent that I got a big mouth, in every sense. Dare I say, the genesis of roachplay? No doubt, my parents were not amused.

5 Sex on foreign soil. Quite literally—it was in an avocado orchard in Israel. Well worth the scorpion bite on my toe and much better than my first sex with a foreigner in Canada. Sorry, Ngweili! tomba.

4 First time at a swingers club. Yes, fourteen heads are better than one.

3 Sex with a woman. (And, yes, she was better than you. Duh!)

2 Public BDSM play. When my soon-to-be master took my hand and asked in the most gentle, paternal way if I'd like to get my ass beat like I owed him money in front of 500 Goths

and kinks…it almost brought a tear to my eye. That might've been because of the Bengay and clothespins he put on my genitals, but why ruin a memory?

1 Pussytoking. Nothing encompasses all that roachplay represents, better; the values of bongslutism; the pinnacle of where sensimilla and safe, sane and consensual meet; an out-of-the-box thinking reader gettin' where I'm comin' from (even if I don't) and turning my goofy ruminations into workable, well-designed reality—that's why I do what I do. And it WORKED. It means at least one of you out there is actually listening and all this alliterated gutterspeak and gonzo googooga-ing isn't for naught. The world should be free to put whatever the fuck they want in their bodies, whether it's dick, drugs or gourd-fashioned paraphernalia. It's okay. I give you permission. Go out and be the best bongslut you can be and remember: Mamakind loves you.

Well…not you. You, I don't like so much.

But you! ***You're golden, baby.***

How Sexy A Stoner Are You?

In the pursuit of happiness, we seek pleasure. Cannabis and skronking are two of the noblest pleasures around and these days, who has time to seek each separately? Balancing your THC/XXX quotient is as important as balancing your checkbook and a fuck of a lot more fun, too.

1. Incorporating ganja and sex is:
    a) Smoking a doobie with yer ole lady, then retiring to the bedroom for some Lynyrd Skynyrd 'n' sweet, sweet love
    b) One word: pussytoking
    c) Jerkin' to "Harold and Kumar Go to White Castle"

2. Your viper hero is:
    a) Jack Herer
    b) Mamakind
    c) Your dealer

3. One of your most beloved strains is:
    a) Passion #1
    b) Fuckin' Incredible
    c) Four-way

4. If your sexual prowess were to be compared to a strain it'd be:
    a) Celestial Temple Sativa—you're strong and keep going 'n going 'n

going...

b) Lowryder—you're short, fat and automatically finish quickly.

c) Donkey Dick

5. The stoner star you most resemble is:

a) Brad Pitt/Megan Fox

b) Dave Chappelle/Queen Latifah

c) David Crosby/Barbra Strei-sand

6. When you want to set the right marijuana mood, you play:

a) "Gin n' Juice" by Snoop Dogg

b) "Sweet Leaf" by Black Sabbath

c) "Don't Bogart That Joint" by Little Feat

7. The sexiest way to get high is:

a) Suckin' on a spliff twisted 'n' licked by a babe

b) Hot knives in the shower

c) One word: pussytoking

8. The perfect pot and sex vacation is:

a) Hittin' Amsterdam for coffeeshops and window hos

b) Bangin' your biatch in the bathroom of every toke-easy café in Vansterdam.

c) Thai sticks 'n' trannies in Bangkok

9. On your night table we'd find:

a) A lamp, alarm clock and glass of

milk

b) Rollies, stash tin and ashtray

c) A Volcano, this book and a
hempen fuck towel

10. Do you consider yourself to be a sexy
stoner?

a) Yes

b) No

c) Sorry, could you repeat that? I
can't hear you over the bubbling of
the buttbong

Key

1. a-1, b-2, c-0
2. a-1, b-2, c-0
3. a-0, b-1, c-2
4. a-1, b-0, c-2

5. a-2, b-1, c-0
6. a-2, b-1, c-0
7. a-0, b-1, c-2
8. a-1, b-2, c-0
9. a-0, b-1, c-2
10. a-1, b-0, c-2

0-10 NOT HOT, POT LAME-O

SWEET MOTHER MARY IN A G-STRING, DO YOU EVER SUCK! And not in a fun way, either. You may love the herb and you may love sex, but you just can't seem to put two and 420 together. Weed for you is about catchin' a glow, not catchin' an STD. You have the sex appeal of Ed Rosenthal and the pot savvy of Sarah Palin. Multitasking marijuana and ma-

kin' whoopee may not be your forte, but at least you can savor each pleasure on an intimate, individual basis.

11-20 SEXILICIOUS STONER

BOO-YAH! There's smoke risin' from your blunt and booty. You easily attend to your hard-on, while gettin' your buzz on. Skilled in the art of roachplay, you live for a good threesome: you, your fuck and your stash. If you could make love to your plants, you'd be the happiest freak ever! The beauty of merging both pleasures is that you attract fellow kind and kindred spirits and together, you'll eventually draw the world to your pot-perverted ways.

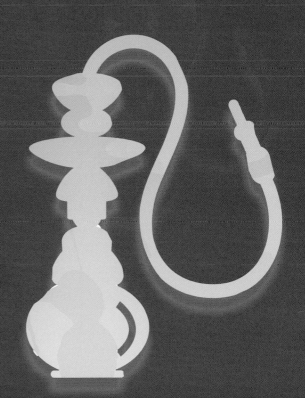

Q Is it weird that I'd rather smoke a bowl than have sex? *Sam Kosho*

I'd rather smoke a bowl of good pot than have some bad sex, if that's what you mean. But generally speaking, yes—it is weird. Why not do both?

Marijuana is a powerful aphrodisiac

Q I have heard many people say that weed is a powerful aphrodisiac, but I was wondering what is in marijuana that makes this possible? Or is it just a lot of concentration on one thing? Also, if there is a certain compound in marijuana that does this, would it not be a good idea to break it down, figure out what it is and maybe make a formula to help people that have a low sex drive? *Jointman*

Marijuana is a powerful aphrodisiac indeed! If it weren't for this fact, I wouldn't be the supreme bongslut that I am today. There are a few chemical reasons why the green makes you want to get it on. Cannabinoids dilate the blood vessels for one, encouraging blood flow that in turn, makes you more sensitive to touch and heat. When blood flows to your bits and pieces, well…you know what that does. Blood flow to the brain stimulates your greatest sex organ of all, encouraging sexy thoughts (increasing dopamine production, making you "feel better") and the uninhibited acceptance of pleasure.

Oxytocin is a hormone stimulated by cannabis ingestion. It works in cahoots with your endogenous or "natural" cannabinoid system. It's both released by your reproductive organs when you get turned on and have an orgasm and it makes your orgasms better by encouraging the muscle contractions that make cum-

ming feel so fucking good. Sometimes called the "cuddling hormone," oxytocin is thought to allow people to feel more trusting and want to spoon after a good skronk session.

What Big Pharma can't put into pill form is the fine, funky feeling that sharing a big phatty with your sugarpie brings. Whether it's because you're already doing something a little "naughty," because such endeavors have you seek out more private settings; or simply because you're spending time together, sharing like interests—there's nothing sexier than marijuana and it won't kill your liver, give you a heart attack or make you see blue. Can't get much better'n that, eh?

Q Could you please settle something between my BFF and I? She says indicas are better for sex and I say sativas are better. There's an eighth riding on this, so we're both anxiously awaiting your answer. Thanks, Mama!
Pugnacious P

I hate to break it to you and your BFF (BTW, I hate acronyms) PP, but you're both right, for three reasons:

- Indicas make fucking more enjoyable by chilling out your mind and body. The cares of the day seem to float off in a puff of smoke, as you lazily (but intensely) enjoy each sensation, your flexibility increased as your muscles relax. Hashish, more often than not made with an indica dom, exponentially increases these effects.

- Sativas can give you some pick-up-and-go, awaken the mind to expressions of passion and creativity and make you feel like dancin' (even horizontally). Your third eye is pried open and sexual energies flow freely throughout your entire being.

- Everyone is different. What works for you may not for me and vice versa. I take that back: everything works for me and seeing as you're both right, you should send me the eighth.

Q First off, just reading your few words in every column gets me off. Keep up the good work. My question is this: if my wife and I get to skronkin' in the ole herb patch, is it possible that the plants might react to the sexual atmosphere created and therefore, stimulate them into a bud frenzy? Of course, the sexual energy will have to be extremely high. Well if you know any info about this, please let me know—or, if you're willing to try this out yourself…? *ogman*

Why—you offering? Without getting too hippy dippy, quantum mechanical, or stepping on *SKUNK Magazine* cultivation editor The Rev's toes—I do believe that flooding your plants with as much positive energy as possible can't be a bad thing (unless you knock over shit while you're doing it). Whether it's

because the hormones you get flowing somehow stimulate similar hormones in your plants (e.g. phytoestrogen); they bask in the light of your shining kundalini as you hump open those chakras; or because you're in such a happy, de-stressed mood afterwards that you pay just a little more attention to your babies—sex and pot are always a winning combo in my nasty lil' black book.

PS–Not enough people use the term "skronkin'." Good on ya', ogman!

PPS–Not enough people use the term "good on ya" anymore. I do, 'cuz I'm the bee's knees.

Are You a Pot Snob?

Everyone has at least one friend (in BC and Oaksterdam, that means all of your friends) who considers him or herself the ultimate cannabis connoisseur. These ganjaphiles would turn down a toke with Moses if it meant sullying their delicate palates with pot that's touched any synthetic matter at all. It's not just a love of marijuana; it's an obsession.

1. When you go to a party, the question you ask most often is:
   a) Who are you wearing?
   b) What are you smoking?
   c) Who are you fucking?
   d) Where's the shitter?

2. Besides weed, the three most important items in your stash box are:
   a) Grinder, papers and filter material
   b) Scissors, papers and a roach clip
   c) Mushrooms, LSD and DMT
   d) Rolling machine, a list of the top three indica and sativa Cannabis Cup Winners for the last four years and a lock of Marc Emery's hair

Ganja Cup Winner

3. S.A.G.E. is:
   a) The name of your hippie babysitter
   b) Society of Americans Glorifying Enema
   c) Sativa Afghani Genetic Equilibrium
   d) Tasty on poultry

4. Someone passes you a joint mixed with tobacco and doesn't tell you first. You:
   a) Politely accept and pass it on. You'll know to pass next time.
   b) Start hacking uncontrollably, pointing your finger and sputtering, "WHICH ONE OF YOU IS TRYING TO KILL ME?"
   c) Pass, sneering and pull out your own pure pre-rolled. Heathens!
   d) Suck it back! Who looks a gift jay in the filter?

5. You're getting married and want to incorporate cannabis in the wedding. You:
   a) Make sure you put aside enough money to buy a zip of the good stuff to share at the reception.
   b) Make sure you grow enough to have a decent pound or two to share at the reception.
   c) Make sure your parents and in-laws are busy doing the Macarena while you go out back with your pals for a quick circle.
   d) Have the bridal bouquet arranged by DJ Short.

6. Your usual method of getting high is:
   a) Whatever green you've scraped together, twisted up in the Zig Zag you found crumpled up under the couch.
   b) Joint, bong, pipe, brownies...who gives a shit? Let's get wrecked.
   c) The best Buddy has to offer in the one-hitter you've had since you graduated high school in `72.
   d) Organic, sixteen-bag processed, reverse-triple-osmosis artesian water extract-ed pre-`98 Lemon Tahitian Trainwreck Super O.G. Silver Temple Haze Kush #5 x Blueberry unpressed hash with a $5000 Volcano Vapo-wand, through a $10,000 ROOR crystalline bong (with charcoal filter, ice holder, ash catcher and nine percolators), served up by Tommy Chong off of Watermelon's ass.

7. Your favorite strain is:
   a) The original Columbian Gold, which you make sure to tell everyone every chance you get just how good it was back in the `70s and bitch about how you can't get it as good anymore.
   b) Whatever you can turn into an

Escalade the quickest.

c) Pre-`98 Lemon Tahitian Trainwreck Super O.G. Silver Temple Haze Kush #5 x Blueberry.

d) Strain? There are, like, different kinds?

8. You'll only smoke ganja that is:

a) Flushed, dried and cured well

b) Grown organically in soil

c) Both a and b

d) Not oregano. You're not gonna fall for that again.

9. You're really desperate for a toke, it's dry everywhere and all your dealer has is shitty, brown brickweed. You:

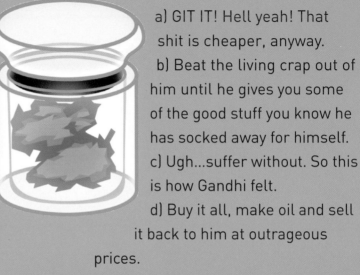

a) GIT IT! Hell yeah! That shit is cheaper, anyway.

b) Beat the living crap out of him until he gives you some of the good stuff you know he has socked away for himself.

c) Ugh...suffer without. So this is how Gandhi felt.

d) Buy it all, make oil and sell it back to him at outrageous prices.

10. The famous pot celebrity whose style yours most resembles is:

a) Jack Herer—you're a tireless activist who won't rest until it's legalized! Good luck in getting someone to name a strain after ya, Herschel

Blatstein.

b) Mr.Nice—you'll tackle international hash smuggling once you get a handle on getting some to your cousin across town, without your snotty bitch sister ratting you out to your parents.

c) Cheech Marin—who? Naw, Dave's not here, man.

d) Bob Marley—at least that's what your seven baby mamas have been tellin' you.

KEY

1. a-1, b-4, c-2, d-3
2. a-3, b-2, c-1, d-4
3. a-3, b-2, c-4, d-1
4. a-2, b-4, c-3, d-1
5. a-2, b-3, c-1, d-4
6. a-1, b-2, c-3, d-4
7. a-3, b-2, c-4, d-1
8. a-2, b-3, c-4, d-1
9. a-1, b-3, c-4, d-2
10. a-4, b-3, c-1, d-2

10-19 points: POT POSER

For fuck's sake! It's just a stupid plant; you don't see what the big deal is. Bud and a Marley means beer and a cig, not weed and a black guy. The important thing is that dirty hippies and college freaks seem to require it to function, so you're that much closer to new Ted Nugent lights for the Chevy.

20-29 points: POTHEAD

Marijuana is fun, although you don't want to get to know it better and take it out for dinner; you just want to put it in you. Lots of it, in any way, shape or form you can. Like a hungry man with a big, barbecued T-Bone in front of him—you don't care where it came from or how it got there; you just think it's a very, very good thing.

30-40 points: AAA PURE ORGANIC POT SNOB

You can name all 64 cannabinoids and your pets are named after several of them. You refer to a strain's legs and flavinoid-spectrum, Robert Connell Clarke referred to you in his last book and you'll see the famous seed breeding family the Dronkers in Thailand for Christmas. You live in Vansterdam, BC and run a vapor lounge and seed bank out of your condo. Someone probably gave you this quiz to make fun of you.

ija Cup Winner

Fetishes andAnal:

Long Live the Kind
& Benevolent Kink

How do you keep from falling off that first step from "handcuffed to the bed," to "suspended from the ceiling with an ice butt plug, pony mask and a needle corset?" That last step's a doozy, fer sher. Kink encompasses an extremely broad spectrum of sexually charged activity. It's like saying, "I want to participate in more sports." You can narrow the field through elimination. Here are some basic categories of kinky activities:

- **Ass play** — Whether it's sticking something (organic or otherwise) in your butt or hers, if there's a hole, you can be sure that it's pleasurable to fill it.
- **Blindfolds and Hoods** — Have a fantasy involving The Unknown Comic?
- **Bondage** — You've dabbled with this, but bondage can be so much more than bedposts and scarves. Shibari is a beautiful form of Japanese bondage. Try materials other than rope to keep someone from wigglin' away: plastic wrap, tape (get the kind that doesn't stick to skin), padded restrains, neckties—hell, even socks. Keep a sharp pair of scissors at hand, just in case.
- **Collars and Corsets**
- **Pain Play** — This is the S&M (sadism (giving pain) and masochism (receiving pain)) in BDSM. Percussive play involves hitting, spanking, caning, whipping, flogging, smacking, etc. Non-percussive includes: pinching, needle and knife play, poking, tickling (if it's to a painful extreme), electrical play, twisting, clamps, ice, wax and fire, hair pulling, etc.
- **Exhibitionism** (showing off) and **Voyeurism** (watching)
- **Humiliation and Begging** — This psychological pain play includes cuckolding (forcing your partner to watch you have sex with someone else), puppy and pony play (just like

it sounds—giddy up!), objectification (treating someone like an inanimate object, like a table or chair), orgasm control, chastity, queening (a woman sitting on a man's face or head), etc.

- **Body Worship** — Bow down to my cock, bitch!
- **Breast Play**
- **Gags**
- **Massage**
- **Role-playing** — This includes costumes and uniforms and all sorts of pretend scenarios like teacher/student, doctor/patient, cop/sexy pot dealer, etc.
- **Toys** —Such as vibrators, dildos, butt plugs, etc.
- **Rubber, Latex, PVC**

- **Stockings, Pantyhose and Shoes**
- **Watersports** — Peeing on or being peed on is an inexpensive way to add, um….spice. Okay, this is kinda gross. But it's certainly not very hazardous to your health (unless you're drowning someone in it) and if it does it for you, then go ahead.

Just remember: safe, sane and consensual. Use "safe words" that alert your partner that you need the play to stop immediately, which partners must respect. Open your mind, heart and mouth to communicate with and you'll open up your sexual horizons.

A Good Helping of Fetish Salad

What's interesting about a den of almost-fanatical conservatism, like my home province of Alberta, is that under its dull veneer, it's almost always rank with twisted underground debauchery of the most extreme sort. Think Victorian England, where piano legs were covered so as not to offend delicate sensibilities (I, myself, go into uncontrollable fits of orgasmic pleasure when I stumble upon an unsheathed oboe). Yet some of the nastiest porn ever written came from

that era. We're talking everything from bestiality to incest; you name it—animal, vegetable, or mineral—the Victorians probably fucked it. Or at least wrote about fucking it.

What about the Japanese? As a culture, they're a pretty staid, mild, straight-laced bunch. But behind the polite bows, rockabilly pompadours and Totoro-emblazoned rice paper screens, they're dirtier than a hobo's nutsack. Any nation that comes up with bukkake, schoolgirl virginity vs. alien tentacles and the cramming (and subsequent gushing explosion) of a thousand live eels into a young woman's anal cavity to the tune of "The Overture of 1812,"

> **Bukkake: a pornography style where a person, usually a woman, is ejaculated on by several men.**

definitely would fall into the "Country o' Freaks" category.

Of course not all fetishes are grounded in sexual repression. But my experience has suggested the very kinkiest of midnight kinks tend to spend their nine-to-five wearing costumes of frustrated banality.

I know a very sweet older gentleman who looks like somebody's grandpa, with his white hair and gentle eyes. You see him and you immediately want to sit on his lap while he tells you a bedtime story or talks about oatmeal.

Incongruously, further investigation reveals that he's double-pierced both nipples—himself—and has a thing for tying up the willing and beating them with bamboo canes like they spit gum on a Singapore sidewalk.

One of my friends dated a pretty little fashionista who sold Prada purses and Manolo Blahnik shoes in an upscale department store by day, but after hours, she got off by being screwed from behind while she puked her guts out. I shit you not. Hey—my friend said that at least that shit was tight...what with her pussy contracting every hurl and all.

Sorry…was that too much information? Well, fuck you. You wandered into the wrong book, my dear, violated, vanilla reader. But I bet you can't help yourself.

to hide it from the outside world, or risk losing everything dear to me: my family, my friends, my freedom. Apparently, what gives me a tiny girlie woody is so perverse and heinous, that its discovery

> **The very kinkiest of midnight kinks tend to spend their nine-to-five wearing costumes of frustrated banality.**

You're going to finish reading this book against your better judgment, aren't you? I bet you are, you dirty little birdie.

Ironically, the fetish I have is the most taboo to the Fox News-watching, Sarah Palin-sympathizing, white bread median masses—illegal, even—and is not really that nasty at all. I still have

by the authorities has caused me to be barred from entering the United States.

Just because I, like many of you, get turned on by the scent of a garden-full of Northern Lights #5 x Blueberry—the curl of smoke that escape my lover's lips after hitting a hash bowl on an exquisitely crafted bong, the warm and tingly high that makes my head float and my Martha sing.

Marijuana turns me on and I know I'm not the only one. These days, with Adam Lambert shmooshing a leashed dude's face into his crotch and Hannah Montana hitting the pole (both on prime time network TV) surely my wee pot peccadilloes wouldn't shock or offend Mom and Pop America at this point, no?

Sadly, you won't be seeing Lil Jon's nipples in an overt simulation of roach-play on the Grammys anytime soon, I guess. Why not? I'll never know.

At least I can expose you all to my kinkiest of fetishes and I know it will

be appreciated, if not practiced. Thank you sweet voyeuristic reader, for making me comfortable enough to express what a truly sick puppy I am.

Q **My query is this: from a woman's perspective, what is the best way to bring up bondage? I have been into the ropes and whips for about a year or so now and have had mixed reactions upon divulging my sexual adventures. How would a woman like to hear it?** *Mojoe*

As a fellow kink, I feel your pain you knotty boy, you—and it makes me so fuckin' hawt, yo! A dom (domme if you're a woman) or top can introduce BDSM-lite actions like hair-pulling and light spanking, all the while querying the bottom with, "Do you like that, baby? Does this make you hot? Do you want me to stop, slow down or keep going?" It'll be apparent whether or not she digs it by her either telling you so, or making it obvious with her body language. Subs should humbly beg, "Please pull my hair/whack my ass," and again, take note of the reaction. If these forays are successful, you should bring it up when you're not having sex. Talk as explicitly as possible about what both your likes and dislikes are. If you do plan on playing, make sure you use a safe-word and follow the golden rules of BDSM: no matter how you're playing or with whom, it must be SAFE, SANE and CONSENSUAL. Happy flogging!

Q Sometimes, when I'm about to reach orgasm, my chick likes to spray me using the fire extinguisher. It's refreshing at the height of sexual pleasure. Plus we get a discount since we refill it all the time. Is this normal and/or dangerous? It's a class two extinguisher. *alibaba*

There is no normal and it's only dangerous if she's sticking the nozzle up yer arse (I can't think it's too healthy to be breathing that stuff, either). FYI, fire extinguishers come in six classifications in North America: "A" for ordinary solid combustibles, "B" for flammable liquids and gases, "C" for electrical equipment, "D" for metals, "K" for cooking oils and "S" for stupidfuck stoners who leave their Nag Champa burning after they pass out. So there.

Q Okay, here's the deal: I'm male and I have this favorite fantasy. See, I find the idea of very tall women extremely arousing. And I mean tall. Say, nine feet, twelve feet. I'm talking can't-happen-in-real-life giantess. I don't understand the origin of this fantasy/fetish and I sometimes wonder if this means I'm a girly man. Conventional bondage-type domination stuff does nothing for me, but I just get totally turned on by the idea

of an enormous woman—a giant-ess who can have her way with me in a gentle, nonviolent manner and who gets a charge from her position of power over me and who is also turned on by my adoration of her and the pleasure I get from her/give to her and over which she is in total control. I've only told a couple women and in each case they were turned off and thought I was a weirdo, so I keep it to myself for the most part. But I could think of some fantasy role-playing with the right partner that would elicit this fantasy and wonder if it's possible that any woman would find this in-triguing at least and fun at best. Or, if maybe it's best I keep it to myself. So, am I a weirdo wussy-man or what?
Lil Lover

Naw, a wussy-man would want a gargantuan she-beast to have her way with him while he was wearing OshKosh B'Gosh corduroy overalls and listening to Death Cab for Cutie.

There's absolutely nothing wrong with this fetish whatsoever. It's not even the weirdest I've heard of (jebus, don't ask). Maybe it stems from being a baby and having women googoogaga over you with their breasts bobbling in your face; perhaps you're really a hobbit. As long as you're not stalking the Cirque du Soleil stilt-walker that lives two doors down, or approaching women in bars on your knees…I'd say you're just fine.

If you have some particular role-playing scenarios in mind and think your new relationship is solid enough to bring out the weird stuff, then go ahead and ask her. It's one thing if she politely declines, but if she puts you down or is rude about it, I'd really think twice about continuing a serious thing.

You're not the one with an issue—she is. Even the most off-put lover should be willing to try—even once—to fulfill her partner's deep-est fantasies. It's the trying that will mark that one as a keeper—not whether or not she successfully pulls her role off.

The Pussytoke Anthology Part I

Okay, it's no string theory, but this is where two green cookies, a hit or three of Indian opiated hash and a lapful of NYC Diesel takes me.

I'm sure you've heard the urban legend about the woman who's rushed to the emergency room with a wine bottle suction-cupped to her cervix. Couldn't the same principle apply to taking a vaginal bong hit?

A woman should (with some eager assistance, a long-necked bong, and a good stash of dank nugs) insert the bong into her pussy, light the bowl and then slowly draw the neck out, creating the suction needed to have: a pussy-toke.

Has anyone tried this? I know it isn't a way to get stoned. I have plenty of other orifices for that. Just for fun, y'know? Something to do when you're stoned that looks cool, like street luge. Am I just riffing on a twisted, perverted, waistoid thought? Again?

These are the heady days of *Jackass* and FUBAR. Surely there must be some (albeit rare) chicks in the stoner sisterhood who share the same wondrous Homer Simpson-esque impulsivity, audacious spirit and total disregard for personal safety found in abundance in the unfair sex?

Now, before I get panicked emails and letters from self-proclaimed cannabis/gynecology experts who believe this practice could lead to a horrendous and agonizing death due to a uterine air embolism, I say this:

1) DO NOT TRY THIS IF YOU ARE PREGNANT! Though, when I was preggo, I had a hard time tying my

shoes, let alone maneuver paraphernalia about my delicate orchid.

2) Remember: We aren't blowing air in; we are drawing air out.

This is yet another case where going out with a dealer (I've had the pleasure of a few) is advantageous. They tend to have:

1) Access to the chron: Even if they don't sell it, most dealers have at least a personal line on good bud, and bud that's good enough for my mouth needs to be thrice as good for my golden gulley.

2) Assortment of bong-age. Come on! You've seen the tampon commercials: Every woman is built differently and should, therefore, have an array of bongs to suit her exact pussytoking needs.

I don't think there exists the particular apparatus that would do the trick for me (there ain't enough Pyrex in my local head shop, baby!), but I've noticed that dealers tend to have the expendable cash to blow on something as absurd as a twat-specific bong.

3) Eager assistance: In my experience, dealers tend to lean toward the adventuresome (know any vanilla dealers?), and if it involves pot and pussies and they don't have to leave the basement, well, where's the signup sheet?

My goal is to someday have several dedicated peons who will do my agricultural and sexual bidding. Undoubt-

Stay away from hitting her spine and lower back, but other than that, the ass can take a hell of a beating, as those of you who went to Catholic school can attest to.

edly, at least one of them is going to have some training in photography and glass blowing.

Another variation on the theme (not to be confused with pussytoking) is to fill your lover's velvet champagne flute with distilled water and rig some kind of human hookah. Gravitational challenges aside, this option is less appealing for the outcome of your ladyfriend walking around smelling like smoked salmon. Isn't *Bongwater Douche* the name of Lady Gaga's next CD? If a hottie with glassware bubbling away from deep within her cooch appeals, go to www.beaverbong.com. These kids are serious about their tokin'-sex fun!

Ladies, it does not take Olympian muscle control and a license to participate in these weedy wet wonders (although it may be illegal in several states, even without the ganja.) She-tokers of the world should rejoice in the liberation of your minds, bodies, souls and boyfriends' stashes in the name of adventure and cool girlie pics!

Oh! COCKTOKES! If you have a bong that fits your johnson semi-snug, you could put it in, get hard and slowly pull it out in order to create the suction. You might need a little lube so said salami doesn't stick to the sides, like hot thighs to a vinyl couch.

Are there any brave men out there who are willing to risk getting caught with their cocks in their paraphernalia? What if you underestimate how big you are and get stuck? How hard is it to turn one of those off?

I bet my Martha could out-toke any Richard, any day (you bet that's a challenge).

So good luck to all myth busting or confirming the ever-enigmatic pussy-toke. Remember: don't get the bong water on mom's carpet, take pictures, send them to me and above all, AL-WAYS PLAY SAFE!

Q My wife and I like to play a game. We simply call it "The Smoking Game." How it works is we get a blunt rolled and then get completely naked. Then we sit on the bed facing each other and light it up. When I hit the blunt, she gets to do whatever she wants to me [during the] two to three hits, then I pass it to her. When she hits it, I get to please her however I want. This goes as long as you can hold out, or until the blunt is gone, in which case you just move right into boinking. We both love this game because we both win in a couple different ways: we end up with a nice buzz from the smoke and a nice buzz from each other (if you know what I mean). So I guess my question is, does anyone else play this game? And if so, do they have any smoking games of their own? *Kindbud_1*

Fun stuff! Good times! I love this kind of thing and I encourage all consenting adults to mix taboos wantonly whenever possible. It's so much more fun than smoking pot without having sex, or having sex without smoking pot. Heck, if you can eat some deep-fried Snickers bars and play a round of Texas hold 'em while you're fucking and toking, even better. I've heard of versions of this kind of "roachplay" or "sex games with marijuana," but from this moment on, your version will forever be Kindbud's Kinky Smoking 'n' Toking Freakfest Extravaganja Super Fun Good Time Happy Game, or KKSNTFES-FGTHG—to me. Feel free to use my kicky acronym as required.

Q **I've heard it's easier to pass STDs through anal sex. Is this true?** *Nasty as it is in San Francisco*

You'd think that your poop-chute would be a little sturdier, but it ain't. It's a soft mucous membrane that doesn't take kindly to being battered repeatedly at weird angles nature never intended. Everything inside there is designed to make things go out, not in, so you're going to meet the resistance of clamping sphincter muscles, tightness and friction, which is why it feels so damn good, right?

This resistance can mean minute or not-so-minute tears in the lining of the rectum or in and around the anus. This, literally, opens both partners up to the transmittal of blood-borne diseases and that's why you have a slightly higher chance of catching a nasty through anal than vaginal.

Q I met a girl a few months ago that gets off by having me spank her. I don't mean a little slap and tickle; I mean that she wants her butt to glow like Rudolph's nose. The more I give her, the more she wants. Recently, she brought home leather cuffs, rope, a rattan cane and two floggers as gifts for me. I have tried them on her, but the more I do to her, the harder she wants it.

This girl is soaking wet and actually dripping after a session. The sex after is out of this world. Here's my dilemma: how abnormal is this? Is it dangerous? How far can it go before it is too much?

The more bruises and welts that I give her, the hotter she gets. She walks around for days, naked and touching her bruises and getting horny. Can I get in trouble doing this stuff to her? Should I try and get her help, or should I just take part and enjoy the ride? As I said: the more I do, the more she wants. What do you think, Mamakind? Kindest regards, *Gardener*

I think I got wet just reading your letter and I think you're a great guy for being willing to try something outside of your comfort zone. She's a lucky painslut; not all partners are willing to indulge their lovers' fantasies, let alone

care enough to educate themselves about the possible negative impact (pun fully intended) of such play.

Use safe words (like yellow for slow

down and red for stop immediately) and respect them. As a top, make sure you're paying attention to your bad little girl, because sometimes bottoms get into what's called "subspace," where they're almost delirious with endorphins and they may not realize themselves when things are getting out of hand (i.e.— you're causing permanent damage). Stay away from hitting her spine and lower back, but other than that, the ass can take a hell of a beating, as those of you who went to Catholic school can attest to. It's all about starting off slow and getting to know your play partner and eventually, your fears will disappear with the crack of your whip.

Q My boyfriend of six months wants to role-play when we're doing it. He's 25 and I'm 24, but lately every time we're [having sex], he wants me to pretend I'm aging as he's fucking me. He wants me to describe the changes going on with my body and how it feels. I was okay with it the first couple of times (heck, he does EVERYTHING to make me happy—it's the least I can do), but now he wants me to pretend to grow old every time. He REALLY gets off on it. I'm sick and tired of pretending that I'm an 80-year-old grandmother getting it on with a 25-year-old. I don't want to do it anymore but at the same time, I don't want to deny him something that gives

him so much pleasure. What do I do?
Old Before My Time

Sounds like ya gotcherself a case of age play, though usually it involves someone pretending to be younger than they are (a lil' Lolita action). Role-playing in the bedroom can be a spectacular way of spicing things up. But it's just that—spice. Do you dump the Tabasco on absolutely every meal you eat? You don't have to have JewGut like me for your intestines to revolt after a while. So why would it be okay to act out your fetishes EVERY time you skronk, as enjoyable as they are? Your system needs a rest every once in a while from such rich undertakings; otherwise, they lose their specialness.

Get him to mix it up a bit. Do you have anything you'd like to try? New toys and/or techniques? Or maybe you'd like to act out your own fantasy...don't be shy fer X'ssake. Your man gets off on you having osteoporosis and glaucoma, so I highly doubt you're gonna freak him out with your deep and dark desires. Lay it on him! Fetishes are fine and dandy, as long as they're not imposing upon someone else and it sounds like you need to gently point out the imposition of constantly imitating Estelle Getty. You'll be old soon enough, young whipper-snapper, so gather ye buds while ye may and enjoy the fact that you can't play hacky sack with your tits and you don't actually pee yourself every time you have an orgasm.

Q **Is it wrong for me to want to fuck dogs?** *DogLover*

Yes. Oy…do I really need to explain why? At the very least, a tail wag and face lick is not consent. We'll just leave it at that. *shudder*

Q **OMG, I AM SO EMBAR-RASSED! I found this stash** of porn on my boyfriend's computer. That's fine — I have no problem with porn, per se. Except all of it was fatty porn! All these fat girls with rolls everywhere, some of them looked like they were 400 pounds. It was disgusting. Does this mean he thinks I'm fat? I have a bit of a muffin top over my jeans, I guess, and by no means am I a runway model (I'm 5'6" and 130 pounds), but if this is what he's into and he says he loves me—he thinks I'm fat, doesn't he? *AnnaBanana*

Oh, get with it! If you found a stash of Asian porn, would you question if he thinks you're Vietnamese?

He's a chubby chaser. So what? It's not disgusting unless they're doing something disgusting. As with any fetish, as long as it doesn't overrun your life what difference does it make? I'm surprised you aren't worried about him leaving you for a real chubbo. You oughtta be flattered that you have something else about you that keeps him around, because it ain't your voluptuousness. You ain't fat, you just shallow, AnnaBanana.

Q Don't ask me how I found this out, but I really like putting a finger or something up my ass when I jerk off. Does this mean I'm gay? *Tesla420*

Only if the finger (or something) has to be attached to another guy for you to like it. Congratulations on your discovery, but I don't really want to know how you found that out, thanks.

The Pussytoke Anthology Part II: Mamakind Tokes Up Her Martha

Last week, while trippin' the acid fantastic and staring listlessly at both my beautiful, newly acquired pretty blue bong on my lap and my beautiful, newly waxed pretty pink petunia in my lap for what seemed like hours (in actuality, it was probably about a minute and a half), I suddenly remembered my pledge to investigate the mystery and wonder that is the pussytoke.

My quest was driven by a superb soundtrack: Easy Star All-Star's *Dub Side of the Moon*, a reggae/dub cover of Pink Floyd's classic, psychedelic must-have *Dark Side of the Moon*. Like a Frosted Mini-Wheat, the Floyd appealed to my 'cid-soaked side, while my ganja side was down with the unobtrusive dub down-beat. Three more sticks of Nag Champa to set the proper olfactory tone and I was ready to roll…er, I mean bowl.

I grabbed wet wipes, some dry wipes, rubbing alcohol, my PBB (pretty blue bong), some organic S.A.G.E. and a lighter. After cleaning the neck of my bubbler with the alcohol and my silk-en gorge with the wet wipes I took a massive (oral) hit and preceded to frig myself with the intention of creating natural lubrication.

Mind you I was on LSD, and I kept getting distracted (by things like air) so that part took longer than planned. *sigh* I love science.

After I felt sufficiently sopping, I maneuvered myself into a semi-squatting position then veeeeery sloooowly lowered myself down onto my pretty blue's neck. I sat there for a bit and contemplated the universe. (That's it-no more scientific investigations on acid!) It then occurred to me that I forgot to repack the fucking bowl. Motherfucker! I bet this never happens to Bill Nye The Science Guy.

Now, at that point one would think I took the damn bong out of my snatch to go get the weed. Noooooooooo! "Not I!" said the whacked-out dumbass.

Big sigh

My stash was sitting only a few feet away, so I decided, instead, to hold onto the bong and very awkwardly walk with the thing dangling between my legs like some drunken hermaphrodite. I packed it with the sugar shake at the bottom of my tin so I could do it with one hand. Yo MamaK does have superior muscle cuntrol compared to your average gal, but the challenge of holding a water-filled bong with my love canal while working a grinder spooked me.

After composing myself briefly, I lit the bowl and ever so slowly and evenly, pulled that puppy out and watched.

Nothing happened.

I shoved it back in again and pulled it out with a little more force, watching for the slightest bend in the flame that would signal success. Still nothing.

I then caught a sight of my ridiculous reflection in the window and started giggling uncontrollably. Having already had a tubal legation, I had to remove said apparatus in order to prevent myself from slipping, shishkabobbing my uterus on shards of broken glass56, thus recreating the procedure. That would've been a great 911 call, I'm sure.

So, it didn't work…that time. Perhaps if I'd had a smaller bored bong, or a longer love canal (I guess there's not much I can do about the latter), it may have worked. This definitely warrants more indepth study, for I feel the matter is not sufficiently resolved.

Perhaps we can combine my "Does toking make it easier for girls to jizz?" research with my pussytoke research in a combined academic undertaking, a kind of complex study of stoner sex science never experienced before. Discovery Channel and NatGeo'll be all over this.

You're damn right: I finished off the bowl the traditional way…after my Martha passed, of course. I'd never waste a good bowl. Who you talkin' to, foo? No, of course I didn't clean it off before I took that regular hit. You know Mamakind's that nasty. S.A.G.E. will never taste the same again.

It quite inspired me; I think I'll start a line of snatch-scented paraphernalia for those who like to combine their marijuana and muff. I'll call it Pussy Pipes or Gash Glass or Under My Thong Bongs or something equally pithy and gross.

Q **What is the best position for newcomers (no pun intended) to anal?** *Behind On My info*

Spooning on your sides makes for the least aggressive entry. The bottom should arch her back as much as is comfortable, and if she's a BBW (big beautiful woman—don't tell me you don't hit that when no one's lookin'), you might want to be chivalrous, top, and hold her mudflaps—um, I mean asscheeks—apart while she does the gentle easing of your Enterprise into her worm hole. Lots of love, patience, and plenty of bubblehash will add to the experience.

If the Front Door's Locked

Sweet, sweet arse. There is nary an orifice as intriguing to a man than the puckered, purple, poop petunia, nor two pillowy globes that so enamor, save boobies. For some, it's a toss up: bajungas or bum. Though there's no doubt a hardcore representation of ladies who covet firm, snowboarder and/or skater tush (they do have the sweetest, most grabable), I've noticed in my stoner wanderings that there are definitely more men who are down with the bedunkadunk as the focus of their lust than women. I personally like an arse shiny and round, one I can roll a joint on while s/he's standing up.

In the BDSM world I'm what's known as a...ahem, heavy bottom (PUH-leeze insert "fat butt joke" here. I dare you). The stress of prohibition simply melts away with the cathartic thump of a flogger on my tender, red rump. Over the knee, bound, suspended, splayed, or simply bent over and grabbin' ankle—any and all positions will do. The best is alternating whacks with light caresses and hits from tha bong. Fine hashish loosens both sphincter and morals while heightening both sensation and pleasure.

Salad tossing, or chocolate starfish gorgin', is an acquired taste. My Play-doh factory tastes tangy, so I've been told—like Zesty Doritos. Mmm...as long as it ain't staining your mouth orange, honey. Funny, although I was always comfortable eatin' someone else's brown flower, I always got wiggy when it came to my own—until recently. It took just the right ass master to take command of my dookie tube for me to feel comfortable and even enjoy it.

The thing is, guys, the real reason y'all like stickin' it to her buttered cornhole is because there's something in your own mangina that can give you insane amounts of pleasure. It's called a prostate (sometimes called the A-spot).

Like my mama always says, "The quickest way to a man's prostate is through his rusty bullet wound." My mama is a fount of indispensable information like that. Unfortunately, though blessed with other, more accessible pleasure centers, women don't have a prostate, so we don't have the bung-draw that guys have. That being said, a woman (at least this woman), usually receives most of her pleasure while getting poked in her Multigrain Cheerio because MEN REALLY GET OFF ON IT.

Yeah, you can play with my clit while you bang my back door if it gets you hotter, baby, but I'd rather you just work on your own earth-shattering O, because I love to hear you moan my praises through gritted teeth and feel that warm spurt slick up my insides, like hot wax in a car wash, but then you gotta get outta there 'cause that's a LOADING ZONE (there's parking in the next lot over, thanks).

I've been told my pink-wink is so

tight that Ashley Olsen may have an issue slippin' one in my stink. "May" because of the JewGut I've developed over the last few years (nagging intestinal problems for those of Ashkenazi Jewish descent, caused by genetics and guilt), that hasn't allowed anything more solid than oatmeal to pass through me. And don't you TMI me… y'all have been sharing your nasty bits with me for years.

I suggest you boys ask for help exploring your own…um, areas. No, taking it like only a man can doesn't make you queer. You can't tell me that seeing your Little Lady come at you with a lubed-up strap-on Pleasure Plow doesn't get ya all hot 'n' bothered!

Picture this: after a Centurion of hot knives, I had my lover on his hands and knees, wrists bound to his nipple rings, black candle poised, ready to alternate reach-arounds, finger-fucking and hot wax drizzles. I grabbed the big black freestanding candle. Bad idea. Those puppies build up a lot of wax—about a quarter-cup while we were foolin' around.

HHHHHHEEEEEEEYYYYYYY-AAAHHHHHH!!!!!!!!!

A thin, elfin scream emanated from nowhere and I couldn't for the life of me figure out where the damn wax landed. It seemed to have disappeared. Upon closer inspection, I noticed an almost imperceptible yet perfect black cast of my boyfriend's entire scrotal area. It missed his ass cheeks completely and went straight down his crack. I couldn't have aimed better.

It was fitting karma for the man who purposefully set my pubes on fire. Twice.

Ass play doesn't make you gay anymore than liking blowjobs or eating Brie. Amazingly, it's illegal in several states. How fucked up is that? Then again, so is smoking weed. Lord, the United States is whack...

Just remember my mantra, guys and dolls: INEBRIATE, STIMU-LATE, LUBRICATE. Have a safe word ready (that you'll remember) in case things get a little too intense. Some Temple Balls or Afghani Rub, some rimming and some J-Lube, will make for a memorable evening, indeed.

Happy sodomizing!

No matter what you're doing with whom and in what hole, always practice SAFER SEX, which means changing condoms when going from pussy to ass and vice versa.

Are You a Pot Pimp or a Pot Ho?

Do you ever have your sack o' nuggs make booty calls for you? Do you walk into a room and all the THC gets magically sucked into your vagina? Are hash and ass equally traded commodities on your pleasure index? We always work what we've got, to get what we want. Are you the player or the played? Throw on the '70s funkadelia and take this quiz to find out, male or female, whether you're a slut for the kind—or because of it.

1. You walk into a toking café and immediately head to:

   a) The nearest open table and get ready to order a coffee

   b) The table with the most girls/guys and get ready to flash your stash

   c) The table with the biggest cloud around it and get ready to put on chapstick

2. The best looking weed at the table is always:

   a) Yours. If you don't have the dank, you won't get the skank.

   b) His, but it'll be yours eventually.

c) Someone else's. You're lucky you can get anything.

3. Weed is to sex, like:
a) Night crawlers are to trout
b) Everest is to a Sherp
c) Kumquats are to Dolly Parton

4. You've just smoked your last bowl. That means it's:
a) Time to call your dealer
b) Time to call your sugar daddy
c) Celibacy time

5. Your favorite strain is:
a) Whatever his favorite strain is
b) Whatever her favorite strain is
c) Blueberry

6. A quarter ounce of marijuana costs:
a) Around $70

b) A blowjob
c) You have no fuckin' clue

7. You hate rolling joints because:
a) Your manual dexterity sucks. Bongs are better.
b) It's hard to see what you're doing under the table.
c) It means you don't get to see a girl/guy lick it.

8. The grow room is the perfect place to:
a) Grow pot
b) Make porn
c) Both A and B

9. Someone gives you ganja as a present. You:
a) Share with everyone, pitching in every roll

b) Get hard, thinking of what you can trade it in for

c) Disappear until you run out again

10. You would give:

a) Weed to get sex

b) Sex to get weed

c) Your right nut/tit for either

KEY

1. a) 0 b) 2 c) 1
2. a) 2 b) 1 c) 0
3. a) 2 b) 1 c) 0
4. a) 0 b) 1 c) 2
5. a) 1 b) 2 c) 0
6. a) 0 b) 2 c) 1
7. a) 0 b) 1 c) 2
8. a) 0 b) 1 c) 2

9. a) 0 b) 2 c) 1
10. a) 2 b) 1 c) 0

0-10 Bend over and grab your grinder, POT HO!

You flit like a hummingbird and mooch like a flea from joint to joint, never sparking one of your own. Like a ganja geisha, you use every drop of your sexual wiles to put your fellow toker at ease, thus loosening the stash-strings. You're probably one of the most hardcore potheads around—you can afford to be when it's not your weed you're hooving down. You smoke weed because it makes you horny for the guys/girls with the weed that you otherwise wouldn't be attracted to, but want to fuck, because they have the weed that makes you horny.

11-20 Put a feather in your fedora and light that blunt, 'cause you look like a POT PIMP!

You lay your stash on the table like you're throwing down a ten-inch dick. The stoner's Arthur Fonzarelli, you click your lighter and the POT HOs snap to your side and fondle your heavy, bulging sack. Whether you really enjoy marijuana is beside the point; you love a lady with an oral fetish and a monkey on her back. You smoke weed because it makes girls/ guys without weed horny, who wouldn't other-wise be attracted to you, but want to fuck you, because you smoke weed.

As Time Goes Bi

"Girls…All I really
want is girls.
And in the morning
it's girls,
'Cause in the
evening it's girls."
— Beastie Boys

I admit it. I like girls. I like boys slightly more—I should qualify that—I like dick slightly more than vag. But women have the soft, jiggly jubblies that are so much fun to squish and chew on; like so much candyfloss without the sticky. Boys are the stick left over after the candyfloss, sticky included.

The first girl I ever kissed (I mean REALLY kissed) was in a lesbian country bar in redneck Edmonton, Alberta. Not exactly *The L Word* ambience; I was in town with friends for Pride Parade weekend festivities. Waiting in line for the little dyke's room to relieve a bladder-full of Long Island Ice Tea, I found myself cozied up to the cutest, cheeriest, most pigtailed cheerleader (queerleader?) I'd ever had the pleasure of sharing pom-pom space with. I commented on the coquettishness of her varsity attire and after a coy and quiet thank you, she leaned forward and firmly planted two velvety-soft, pink bowtie lips on mine. I still remember her little tongue prodding my own like a kitten lapping cream; the taste of grape (not cherry, bitch) lip gloss lingering well after I unsteadily returned to the table, forgetting to go pee. And yes, this all happened waaay before Katy Perry got out of elementary school.

For some reason, at that time in my life, ALL my friends were gay—male and female. I dunno—I had a couple of gay roommates, they introduced me to their friends…next thing I know I'm sucking back $1.75 blow jobs at the back shooter-bar and playing Eddy

Love people, not their gender.

in the Boyztown Theatre Players' production of *Rocky Horror Picture Show*.

On a regular basis, my friends would try to goad me into owning a 100% commitment to homosexuality. But alas for them: a large-boned, sexually adventurous, Ani DiFranco-listenin' gal does not automatically a lesbian make.

I had various flirtations with girls throughout my twenties. Ladies lilting in and out of my life—everything from the usual (and probably de rigueur by today's standards) E-induced dance floor make-out sessions, to longer-term relationships resplendent in all the glory and misery that follows. Crushes on chicks…you bet. There isn't a human with working parts, male or female, who wouldn't want just four minutes and twenty seconds with Angelina Jolie's luscious collection of lips.

I've played the innocent ingénue, enraptured by prowling cougars with thick European accents, tattooed eyeliner and the most perfect fake knockers I've ever seen a-swingin' in a swingers' club. I've played the part of a prowler (okay, a cougar cub)—and had the tables turned when the ingénue out-licked, out-fingered and generally outplayed my sad, thirtysomething ass. I grew up with Madonna in "Like A Virgin." She had Xtina in "Dirty." I definitely reaped the benefits of a sluttish teen culture—Generation XXX.

I think girls (or "grrrlz"—oh yeah, I can be fierce too, Avril) today are soooo much more relaxed about their sexual orientation, or rather, we don't peg it to one end of the spectrum or the other too early, thus never revisiting the question. When I was growing up, the only carpet-muncher in my neck of the TV woods was Jo on *Facts of Life* and we were supposed to believe that bitch liked man meat. Now, on the popular Canadian teen show *Degrassi* (first gig of hip-hop artist Drake; like the warm and sunny *OC*, but in cold and dark

T.O. (Toronto, Ontario), there are lezzie teen strippers and polygender bed hopping galore.

Nowadays, we have this "bicurious" label to throw around. Like visiting someone else's church—"I'm switiching because the pews are softer and the hymns peppier." Or, "No thanks; I'm just staying for the Bar Mitzvah. But I might as well get loaded on Manischewitz while I'm here…" I didn't think it possible to be more noncommittal than bisexuality: I can't decide. I like 'em both. With bicuriosity, it's: I can't decide about whether I want to decide. I may like 'em both, or maybe I don't. Maybe I like just one. I can't decide which one,

though. Stop pressuring me! I need a latte….

Guys have it easy. Culturally pandemic homophobia, along with an over-developed sense of neo-polititcal correctness, forces guys to be either straight or gay. Typical—pick a team and stick with it, dammit! It doesn't matter which one, as long as it's the one that wins. Whereas no man would deny himself even the remote possibility that his woman might go porn star on him and will soon be participating in or at least present for some kind of future beaverfest. So dabbling—for women—is encouraged.

My advice for the girl who can't decide which side of the canoe to dip her paddle in: go with what feels right, even if what feels right today, may not tomorrow. Love people, not their gender. Or this: try indica and sativa, even though you have a preference for a body or head stone and you'll find serendipitous experiences hidden in both that you wouldn't have if you had smoked only one.

Q **My dick isn't as big as most guys, but I have a small girlfriend. How can I pleasure her to really scream?** *Jordan*

You can start off by not being so cock-centric. Believe it or not, there are other ways to pleasure a woman than simple intercourse. I can take up a whole book to tell you what makes me cum (*Sex Pot II*, perhaps?), but I am not the petite lady in question (I sure ain't petite and the lady thing is also questionable). The only way to really know what works for her is to go right ahead and ask. Her, not I.

Even better than asking questions is asking her to show you what she likes. Instigate some mutual jackin' 'n' jillin' sessions and while you're getting yourselves off, pay attention to what she's doing to make herself scream. And for fuck sake, learn a bit about female anatomy, so you don't need to slap on a spelunking helmet and grab your GPS every time you're feeling randy. And no, you can't use the word randy and still be cool…unless you're me.

The Hills

Man alive! I luvs me some jubblies.

Fun bags are my favorite female body part—inclusive of pussy. Soft, pliant bajungas not only make you want to screw, they make you want to put your head down and drift off, like a hammock strung between two trees gently swaying in the breeze on a lazy Sunday afternoon. Vaginas just don't have the same "cute factor" that their northern neighbors do. It's the difference between two plump plums and an equally sweet (possibly even sweeter) prune.

> "I wanted to retire from all that, but I guess my breasts still have a career and I'm just tagging along with them."
> - Pamela Anderson

In fact, knockers were designed to make you want to stick your lips on 'em, weren't they? This is also how we know that whatever supreme power of divinity or science came up with the boob, it wasn't male; if it were, women would have at least six of 'em—two to nibble on, two to squeeze and two to fuck.

> **If you own a pair of knockers, or love someone who does: get to know them, take care of them, celebrate them and treasure them**

Speaking of balloon mining—how much fun is that? It's sort of like anal in the way that she really gets off because it drives him so coo-coo, a grit-yer-teeth-'n'-bear-it-for-all-womankind martyr kinda thing. I'm never sure what the best position is for planting a carrot in my melon patch, so I usually end up on my back with buddy straddling my chest. I try to mix it up a bit, throwing a bit o' blow job in, just because his dick's already in close proximity to my mouth. But it ends up being a cross between that retarded party game where you pass an orange to someone without using your hands and trying to suck a popsicle dangled over you by a bungee cord. By the end of the ordeal, he's got a Grand Canyon-sized grin on his mug and I've got two collapsed lungs and an eyeful of splooge.

But if it makes you happy, poopie cakes....

I've gone and decorated my tatas with some lovely tiaras (as opposed to a pearl necklace). Both an aesthetic and physical pleasure, my nipple rings are just rewards for my girls' decades of dedicated service. First as sore, blossoming buds stuffed into a bra at the tender age of nine (which scared the bejebus out of my parents, no doubt envisioning their eldest on the pole at eleven).

I remember wanting them to hang like my mom's and all the other women I knew…who were all moms, too. *heavy sigh* Egad was I a dumbfuck…

At fourteen, I started to "get it:" the power contained in the two lumps of flesh adorning my chest could hold the male species in such sway; a stricken, drooling stupor that could translate into always having someone to dance the slow songs with, much-needed tutoring in math, a nod from the coolest guy in school, or even a free bag of Doritos.

By the time I hit high school, I had mastered my guns and by the time I graduated, I was a black belt in Chachki Fu, delivering devastating TKOs of man manipulation without so much as lifting my shirt, thus exchanging tutoring and Doritos for tequila and engagement rings.

Then they really came into their own: motherhood. I went up to a fuckin' H cup with my first…that's almost freakish. To enhance the situation, three days after women give birth their beach balls get so inflated with milk, they go rock hard and for the first time since I hit puberty, my nipples faced the wall. Holy Saint Anna Nicole! I had porn star-sized happy sacks (periodically spraying a dozen streams of mom juice across the room in random directions, like a ceiling sprinkler)…and no one to appreciate them except my son, whose first memories must be of looking up and seeing Mars filling the sky, crashing into the planet.

So I implore you, if you own a pair of knockers, or love someone who does: get to know them, take care of them, celebrate them and treasure them; be they big or little, round or pointy, firm or soft, parallel with the ground or wall.

Thanks for the mammaries.

Q When I have sex with my girlfriend and take her pants off, a very foul smell protrudes from her vagina. When we have sex she gets extremely wet to the point where it goes all through the sheets and puddles the mattress. Yesterday she got a good amount of moisture on one of my white shirts and stained it yellow. This has been going on for months. She was tested for STDs about a month ago and everything came out negative. This can't be normal. What's going on? *Dating a Fish Market*

I'll have to be honest with ya, D.A.F.M., you came close to stumping yo MamaK here. Close but no Dutch. It could be bacterial vaginosis, which is easily treatable with an antibiotic, but barring that…there could be a couple things at play here.

First off, there's nothing coming out of your girl's pussy that sounds necessarily unhealthy from what you've told me, except Eau du Skank. Puddles of juices ranging in color and consistency from thin and clear to creamy, yellowish beige, will accumulate if you're doing all the right things, so don't worry about that.

Now, about that stench. Why don't you run a surprise bubble bath or grab her ass and head to the showers and re-assess afterward. It could be that your woman's crotch gets a little sweatier

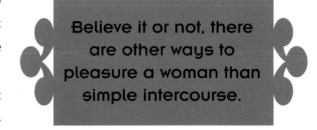

Believe it or not, there are other ways to pleasure a woman than simple intercourse.

and nastier during the course of the day. You don't mention anything out of the ordinary, except the stinkiness, so unless she starts poppin' up symptoms of something else, I am prone to think you have a particular intolerance to her ape-kooze scent. Heavy sessions with strains like Skunk #1 and God Bud before each encounter mean that you won't smell or remember what the problem was in the first place.

Q I'm twenty-seven and have always been really conscious about using safer sex practices. I've always used condoms and never had problems with any brand I've used—until recently. It seems that lately, all of my usual brands leave my pussy sore and swollen after only one go at it. I can usually go through a whole box and still be ready for more. I tried changing lubes and switching to different brands of condoms (the ones I can get at the gas station nearby). By the next morning or within a few hours, everything is back to normal, so I'm not worried about an infection or anything, plus I get tested on a regular basis. This is nuts! It keeps happening, no matter who I'm with. Am I becoming allergic to sex?
Itchy Koochie-koo

Itchiness disappearing shortly after sex tells me you're allergic or sensitive to something, either condoms or him. Ask dude to Axe the noxious body spray, to begin with. Barring that, while developing a man juice allergy can and does happen, it's most likely an allergy from using condoms.

Eliminate Nonoxynol-9 spermicide. This shit causes itchiness and has been blacklisted because it extends the life of the HIV virus, putting you at risk, even after the rubber comes off. It's not unusual to develop latex sensitivities or outright allergies over time, narrowing which love gloves you can use to just a few brands. You'll need a full-on drugstore or, if you should be so lucky to have one in your area, a condom boutique. More expensive, yes, but suck it up gimp, or you might as well enter the convent now.

Low-protein condoms are latex, but with less irritants and are most commonly used in porn today. Slip one on and feel like a pro! Polyurethane is stronger than latex, thinner and transmits heat better, but it's not as elastic. Female condoms are made from polyurethane, too, but use Nonoxynol-9 and some complain that it's like fucking a Ziploc baggie.

Natural Lambs are made from lamb intestine and if animal guts in your snatch aren't allure enough, they're only good for preventing pregnancies, not STDs.

Finally, avoid irritating glycerin-based lube. Get water-based (hemp lubes are water-based), because anything else eats holes in most condoms and some of your toys, too.

Pussytoking Part III: Ain't No Bongslut High Enough, Ain't No Pussy Deep Enough

If you've read this book thus far, you'll be fully aware and mostly likely sitting in tempestuous anticipation of the next (and sadly, final) installment of the infamous Pussytoker triptych.

In our first segment, I introduced you to the wondrous phenomenon of pussytoking; we discussed how the idea is based on the urban legend of the unfortunate damsel who landed herself in the ER with magnum of Dom suction-cupped to her cervix. Could we then use the same principle to take vaginal bong hits?

"For why?" you ask, in fairly bad English. For to—because—you can. It makes for YouTube-material so fantastical, it'll knock *Two Girls, One Cup* into distant, sickening memory.

Because you want to show off what a tremendous bongslut you are.

Because, although a piss-poor way of getting stoned, you want to prove that every mucous membrane of every orifice is dedicated to the ongoing quest to get fucked, in every sense of the word.

Because I told you to, dammit. Listen to your Mama!

The second column in the illustrious series saw an attempted self-realization of a dream—albeit a failed one. I put bong to cunt and finger to keyboard to introduce my Martha to my pretty blue bong. Unfortunately, the copious amounts of LSD and bad genetics (mine, not the ganja's) coursing through my veins kinda put a kibosh on the whole shebang. Either the PBB was too long, or my cooze too short…that's what I kept telling myself, anyway.

Enter Canadian punk gourd artist—yes, gourd—Steve Genereaux of Ontario's Unconventional Art. Steve takes the lowly, hollow gourd (sorta like a pumpkin) and turns it into a thing of beauty and utility: bongs, bowls, pipes and (my favorite) gourdildos—a great porn name, to be sure—which are just as they sound: dildos and butt plugs made from Mother Nature's veggie pottery. In fact, you've probably seen his bong emblazoned with a glow-in-the-dark Sparky—*SKUNK Magazine's* mascot—a couple of times amongst their pages.

I've known Steve for a while; he's always been an awesome supporter who I've had the pleasure of partying with in person. He even blessed me with the prototype gourdildo, Big Blue (it's as long as a baby and as thick as my farm girl wrist).

Shortly after the first column came out, Steve swore to me, having worked as an industrial designer for years, that he'd design a real pussytoker (I love using the word industrial and pussy in the same sentence). I thanked him for putting that much effort into thinking about my goofy idea for longer than an hour, which is probably fifty nine-and-half minutes more than it deserved. I honestly didn't expect that he'd remember it, much less attempt to make one.

Then, lo and behold: a humble brown box, slightly smaller than a breadbox, arrived labeled *Attn: Mamakind*, about a year-and-a-half later. I was astonished to pull out what appeared to be the world's first pussytoker. A palm-sized, hourglass-shaped gourd is fitted with a glass bowl. Rubber surgical tubing leads to the bottom of a dildo-shaped gourd with a tiny, peehole-lookin' hole at the other end. It brought tears to my eyes and wetness to my crotch. There were even instructions! I was so excited to try it I almost pulled it out on the bus home.

Fast forward a few hours, after the chilluns have hit the sack and there is no risk of pussytokus interruptus. I call upon my many years of experience in stoner doofusdom and set the mood:

Nouvelle Vague—a little bossanova to soothe my bubbler hittin' blambooey. I was going to use *Three Times a Lady*, but I don't like to touch my split peach to Lionel, ever since that easy listenin' scored gangbang in 2001.

I pack the bowl with some sugary, pre-ground White Widow and detach the hose from the nipple (I love that word). With my man's eyebrow-cocked help, I insert the dildo end (essentially, the mouthpiece), put the hose to my mouth and light the bowl to "prime the pump." Once the tube is milky with smoke, I quickly reattach the hose to the inserted "pussy piece" and slowly pull it out.

The moment of truth is at hand… and the tinniest tendril of smoke puffs out of my vajayjay.

Good enough for me—success! Never mind that I couldn't duplicate the wisp after trying again for another twenty minutes or so. Never mind that I had to stop because my juices were clogging the hole, or that I hadn't waxed, so samsquanch sandwich pictures were out of the question.

It worked.

Thank you, Steve, for turning my psychedelic ruminations into reality.

You're a gourd man.

Q **How do I make my girlfriend cum?** *Jake*

Jebus, Jake! Do I know your girlfriend? How do you make her cum? Or how do you make her cum? I'm a fucking stoner, man; stop asking me all these complicated questions. Sheesh.

I would try asking her flat out: "What makes you cum?" If she's not willing to tell you, ask her to show you. If she's not willing to do that, then perhaps making her cum is the least of your worries and you should be asking her if she's in the market for another boyfriend.

Finally, don't concentrate so much on making her cum. Some women can't seem to figure out how to make themselves cum well into middle age and pressure from their partner doesn't help. If you find that's the case with your girlfriend, encourage her by helping her to explore the possibility of an orgasm with her, following her lead.

Always be supportive, encouraging and loving and the answer will become apparent.

Q **I love giving my hen oral sex, but she just don't let me go down as often as I like. What can I do to make her more receptive?** *Catdaddy*

It's a bit difficult to say without

knowing her personality. Do you know why it is she doesn't enjoy a good carpet munching? Is it because she doesn't like the sensation (granted, the least likely reason)?

When I was younger, it wasn't my favorite either, because I experienced some real droolers. I mean, these guys slobbered so much that it felt like a bull mastiff eating pudding between my legs, and contact couldn't be made between tongue and Martha, so it just tickled and weirded me out.

Perhaps, you're not using enough lubrication and it's painful; some women can't stand direct contact on their clits and you need to concentrate on the hood, or some other bit nearby. Perhaps, someone once told her that she smells, so she's now self-conscious. A good habit to get into is for both of you to shower, or bathe, before you get down and dirty (or take it together and save some time). That can alleviate any fears about the stank of the day getting' in the way, and if you both do it, no one will feel bad (you might have a certain ape scent going on, with which she's just putting up).

Maybe, she's afraid you might expect the favor returned and she doesn't like sucking wang. Maybe—and this one actually happened to me—you're just too into cunnilingus and she wants something different. I once dated this guy who had such a pussy fetish, he'd wear me as a hat if he could, and while it was fun for a while, it started to get tiresome (not to mention, my kaslopas felt like steak tartare).

I just wanted to be fucked—is that so wrong? Once you've diagnosed the problem, then you can tackle it head-on (pun fully intended).

Ask her flat out and don't be pushy if she doesn't want to answer and, for fucksake, don't ask her while you're having sex, unless you want an instant mood killer. Ask her what she does want and you crazy kids will be just fine.

Q OK, so I was watching some porn the other day and some chick squirted cum out of herself! It was the most awesome sex thing I've ever seen. My question is how the hell can I get my girlfriend to do that? Can all chicks do it? You gotta tell me how, please! *Girlspuzz Neophyte*

Indeed, if your lil' lady is anatomically correct she should be able to spew her womanly spunk.

Female ejaculation happens when the urethral sponge (a.k.a. the G-spot)—which is located about an inch or so up and toward the front of the vaginal wall and the urethra (a.k.a. the pee hole)—is stimulated, swollen with fluid (not pee) and squeezed out, redefining "the money shot."

Firm "come hither" action with two fingers on this spongy patch while you're lightly licking or playing with her clit with a vibrator will bring forth the necessary G-spot orgasm required. As she gets ready to cum and the urethra fills up, that's when she's gotta trust that even though it feels like she is gonna piss herself, she's just gotta go with it.

As she bears down and uses those same PC pee muscles, she should burst forth a gush, dribble, spray, or stream of milky white to clear liquid and it should feel MAH-VELOUS!

Skill In Jackin' 'n' Jillin'

Excuse me…I need to wash my hands. Okay, that's better—my sexslick fingers were mucking up the keyboard.

I came across a study that said that approximately eighty-nine percent of women and ninety-five percent of men have masturbated. Are the other eleven and five percent lying? Duh! I've had a few women tell me they've never rubbed one out and one told me she's never even put her finger in her pussy. I think that's total and utter bullshit—how does one have a hole in one's body for one's entire life and not stick their finger in it, at least once? Especially as a kid (kids stick their fingers in anything that doesn't have a whirling blade and often that isn't even a deterrent.)

Another friend (where do I meet these women?) said that she's never even seen her own hoohoo before. Not even in the fuckin' mirror. That's insane. How is that possible? That's like saying you've never seen your belly button (I call my belly button "the Abyss.") She said she never had the desire to look and even seemed a little grossed out by the thought. My GAWD.

I've practically lived in mine my whole frikken life. I know my twat so well inside and out; I could make you a Fimo model to scale in about four minutes and twenty seconds.

The only ones who are as acquainted with my snatch as I are the small battalion of OB/GYNs I've dealt with over the years and one of my exes, who was so obsessed with my cunt, I thought he'd sublet his apartment and move into it.

As with anything really fun having to do with the body, it's that gosh darn Western religion that's made shameful one of the most beautiful processes in nature. The gift of self-pleasure is one that we can make use of at any time, in any place, save for decency, lube and the weather. I've rubbed one (or two, or three) out in some pretty crazy places:

- On a bunk bed in Jerusalem
- On the floor of a downtown office building
- On Astroturf on the front porch at six in the morning
- In an avocado orchard
- In a small movie theatre during some piece of crap staring at that Belgian kung fu idiot
- On the outside deck of a BC ferry
- Waiting for the bus on the highway across from a prison at an Army personnel drop-off point somewhere in Butt-Fuck-Nowhere, Israel, while people walked past with Uzis and M16s
- On a float house
- With three other men "asleep" in the same room
- In the front seat of his daughter's really old car
- In Northern Alberta in December, in a car, next to an oil pumping station
- In a restaurant kitchen
- On an elephant in India
- In Vancouver City Jail
- In the highlands of Scotland amongst the heather

> As with anything really fun having to do with the body, it's that gosh darn Western religion that's made shameful one of the most beautiful processes in nature.

- While waiting at the passport office
- Hands-free while driving
- Mitchell, South Dakota
- Whilst writing the table of contents at *SKUNK* headquarters

Sometimes it was a group experience; more often than not it was a solo venture.

Orgasms raise dopamine levels, making you feel better than the muscle contractions alone could. I know that if I have a hard time getting to sleep (I tend towards nasty cases of Sunday night insomnia) I can reach down and pet kitty until I'm overcome with that lovely post-coital sleepiness that doesn't have to involve coitus at all. However, I do get a little miffed at myself afterwards for just rolling over and going to sleep without so much as an, "I love you, Mamakind," or a spooning sesh. Damn, I can be such an insensitive bitch.

Whether or not you're skronking on a regular basis, you really do need to take the time to explore—on your own—what makes your body tick 'n' groan. How the hell do you expect somebody else to know that you hate having your dick rubbed without lube, but you'll mew like a kitten if your balls are jingle-jangled with one hand, while the other whacks at the speed of sound using the two-finger-and-thumb medium grip method?

Why would anyone know that you'll hit the roof if your clit's touched directly, but you'll squirt like a fountain if you get fucked with three fingers and a dildo up your ass?

With all the talk of STDs, unwanted pregnancies and general sexual stigma, you should be the first person you turn to satisfy your most basic of needs along with food, shelter and marijuana. And if you can't satisfy the sex-fiend looking back at you in the mirror, then you'll never be the "whole" person of the two "whole" people that make up each half of a successful relationship.

Love thyself…and make love to thyself soundly.

When is a dick not just a dick? When it's a few of many erogenous zones. Think of his entire genital area as a keyboard; it's 1982 and you're Thomas Dolby. Men have a whole bunch of love buttons and if you learn to work them right, you'll be blinding him with sighs in no time.

The A-Spot: Hidden in the depths of every man's rectum is a special nubbin of love about the size of a walnut—the prostate. It's reached by similar methods to the G-spot on a woman, but in his mangina instead. With a condom and much lubrication over an index and middle finger (trim those nails, girls), play around the asshole until it's relaxed enough to allow easy insertion of one, then two fingers (this may take a minute or two). You'll feel another ring of muscles about two inches up the rectum. It'll take a minute or so for those muscles to relax and then, when the fingers can go up about three or four inches, crook them toward the cock and gently stroke. It's firmer than the surrounding area and very sensitive. Getting a hummer and/or being jacked off at the same time adds to the excitement. But trust me, don't let him hold your head while he's doing it or he'll rip it off when he cums.

The P-Spot: The perineum or "taint" ('taint yer balls and 'taint yer ass) is an inch-long area between his asshole and ballsack that's a veritable runway of love. Gently kneading, pressing, or rubbing the P-spot can trigger some guys to cum.

The F-Spot: This is the loose (and very sensitive) little doohickey of skin under his cockhead, where the head meets the shaft. Gently rub it using your thumb with some lube or spit and he may start bleating like a lamb.

The R-Spot: This is the visible (and highly sensitive) line along the center of his sack.

Q I'm eighteen years old and a virgin. Yeah, that's right—a virgin! The reason I have this problem is because of a shortage in penis size. I've been with my girl since April 20th and we still have yet to have sex. She knows I'm a virgin, too. She's starting to ask me why I don't want to have sex with her, or let her do anything to me. But I don't know how to tell her and I think this chick could be the perfect bowl to my downstem. All I want is to lose my virginity, but I don't know if I can keep her waiting much longer (the good thing is, she's being pretty patient).

So, if there's any advice you could give me, or secrets to make my penis grow, let me know; I don't have enough money to buy penis enlargement supplements. *Lil man*

Aaaawwww! That's the cutest little— "the perfect bowl to my downstem"— that's so sweet! Technically, though, the bowl fits into the downstem, so you're the bowl and…never mind.

I get the "my dick's too small" question a lot and nine times out of ten, it's totally unwarranted. Your dick's prolly just fine (five inches is the U.S. average, with wood). It certainly shouldn't keep you from gettin' your cherry popped. You just need to be more comfortable in your own skin. Try dimming the lights and popping in a porn for a mutual jacking 'n' jilling session.

Don't even touch each other. She'll probably see it first when it's nice and hard, anyway, so it'll be more impressive and you can both pick up visual tips on how to please one another that aren't so intercourse-centered.

Move from pleasing yourselves, to pleasing each other the same way. Once you've cum a couple of times in each other's presence, the natural flow of things will have you canoeing in her waters in no time and she won't give a shit what size your paddle is.

Getting Ahead in Getting Head

I've worked very hard at perfecting my "back of the tongue/soft upper-palate head squeeze" technique. Twice I've metalicized my tongue so I don't have to use my hands. Ahem.

MEN: Look for the girl who's a hard bong hitta' and can't roll a decent joint to save her life. THC + Oral Fixation + Large Lung Capacity + Poor Manual Dexterity = Stonerchick Who Gives Killer Hummers.

WOMEN: If you can put up with a bruised throat and his wad shooting very quickly elsewhere than your snatch, wear pigtails or braids and let him grab hold like a Harley and bang the shit out of your face. This appeals to so many men on so many levels. Plus you'll feel all cute and "take-able."

A guy once fucked my head like that in a pool. It's a good thing I was a synchronized swimmer and tuba player and now I'm a super-chronic toke-monster…I hold my breath like a pearl diver.

My relatively few wang tootin' issues are:

Smeg. Penis butter. Head cheez. Whatever you call it, it's tre sick. Props to my 'Brews in tha hood; I've never slurped a meat popsicle that was circumcised and makin' dick pate (it just ain't kosher).

Men who never pop. Trust me, this isn't the time to practice your Tantric seed withholding, Sting. I have a (albeit velvety) log repeatedly blocking my airways, penile induced TMJ, a pube giving my uvula a goatee and I just want you to moan my praises and then return the favor, sweetie. Please come…for me?

Jizz up my nose. Poor little wigglers, they must be so confused: "Pink, dark, warm, wet—fuck! I know that egg's in here somewhere…!" Meanwhile, I'm blowin' paper-mâché out of my sinuses for hours.

Save the Skin for Me

Oh dear. I hope my previous comments didn't offend those whose hummer hummus-free tubesnakes still wear high turtlenecks…why, I even married an un-pruned man.

Foreskins are really great to play with and chew on; more akin to an inner labia than an outer one…but sometimes you have to hold it out of the way—like a window blind that won't stay down.

Suckin' back a long, warm one

A friend of mine saw a girl at an orgy ask someone for his condom after he spuzzed in it and then she proceeded to SUCK THE SEMEN OUT OF IT! Like a package of relish. EEEeeeww-ww…I don't know why this grosses me out so much; the same splooge could be shot down my throat from the source and it wouldn't bother me at all.

Some women are totally icked out by a shot o' man juice. However, if you are one of those flowers with a delicate constitution, it is only polite to help your paramour "get rid of the evidence." Hear that, Lewinski?

If you don't want to have to clean it off the wall (or get it in the eye) and you won't provide a proper flesh receptacle, then Mistress Manners says it is proper fellatial etiquette to hold your hand over his cannon when it goes off. It's much easier to wash your hand than to have to comb O-snot out of your do, so sayeth Cameron Diaz.

It is definitely NOT acceptable to pretend to swallow and then spit it out onto his stomach. Unless he's into that, I guess.

Jesus-Christ-with-an-ice-hooter— just swallow it, you silly bitch! One, maybe two gulps of chlorinated, salty skim milk (unless he's been into the garlic). Only six calories per teaspoon…like a Tic Tac!

A big hit off the Super Lemon Haze cone he rolled will take care of the taste. Good thing, 'cause you can't roll worth shit.

Q **I'm afraid to give my boyfriend a blowjob, but he always wants one.** *howydavies*

Okay, sweetie…can you explain to me what you're afraid of? Are you afraid because he always wants one? Because I can tell you right now, he always will.

Now, I've seen some freaky-ass members in my time, but I can't say I've ever seen one that made me scream (at least not in fear); there've been some that made me laugh, regrettably.

Are you afraid of choking? We should all be so lucky to be confronted with so thick a one-eyed monster!

Here's a tip to keep from choking on that whole two tablespoons or so of jizz: when you think he's gonna cum (his balls might get tight or he'll grab you by the hair and go, "Thar he blows!"), stick the tip of your tongue over his pee hole, let the splooge collect in your cheeks and when he's done writhing, it goes down in one quick, painless, watered-down Elmer's glue gulp.

> I'm a strong proponent of swallowing. No muss, no fuss, no presidential impeachment.

Q **Why don't women swallow? I mean…uh, what's the big deal?**
The Hun

Regular readers of my writings will know that I'm a strong proponent of swallowing. No muss, no fuss, no presidential impeachment.

Women who refuse to swallow do so because they're grossed out. I don't think it takes a sex columnist and a congressional hearing to figure that one out. Why are they grossed out? It's the taste, the texture and/or the entire idea of someone's body fluids shooting down her gullet. Or it's a combination of all three.

I'll repeat this for all of you who smoke the good stuff: if a fellatist finds herself gagging at the sheer force and quantity of your manly gush, she can try waiting until you're just about to cum (a tap on the shoulder, or, "I'MGONNACUMFUCKYEAH!" should suffice), then place the back of her tongue against your urethra, letting it spurt into the sides of her mouth where she can store it in her cheeks until you're done ejaculating.

She can then quickly (and unnoticeably) gulp what ends up being not more than a couple of tablespoons down, at her leisure, without making off-putting or unseemly faces. Try laying off the garlic and flesh, though—wan, sensitive, emo vegans who call black pepper spicy do taste better.

Q My girl recently went on a new diet and while she's on it she won't go down on me because she's afraid of the damn calorie count!! It's not just the same if I can't get at least one nice, wet, sloppy BJ but the new diet has her mouth clamped tight and unfortunately I'm not in it!

How many calories are there really in a typical cum shot, how much exercise would it take to work off those calories and is there a typical food that has about the same calories that she could just avoid afterwards that would make up for being a great girlfriend? *Delta 9*

Will wonders ever cease? You know women are too diet-crazy when…

First off, remember that semen is ninety percent water and the average size load is approximately five cubic centimeters. That's four-and-a-half cubic centimeters of water, which has no calories. How can a half cubic centimeter of anything have that many calories?

Male jizz has the approximate composition to that of a chicken egg white, only about one-seventh the nutrients. Therefore, a shot of man juice has about two calories and a tenth of a gram of protein. If your girlfriend cuts one egg white out of her diet, it'll be worth a week of hummers. It probably takes more than two calories to roll a joint, pack a bowl, or suck your weewee for that matter, so she's got no excuse. You win—and you owe me big time, Delta 9.

Q **Do girls like big dicks or small dicks? My girlfriend broke up with me because she said she wanted a guy with a smaller penis.** *Hooden*

I am sorry you misunderstood, Hooden. She actually said she wanted a guy who wasn't such a big dick, not a guy who had one. Ba-dum-dum.

Q Can you tell me what's the best way to get my penis to stop humming when the lights go out? Every time the room gets dark, my penis makes a humming sound. I don't know what to do. I'm too shy to go to the doctor. My lover finds it funny, but I think it's annoying. I can't sleep—it hums! ((EvIL))

Put earphones on your Johnson and let him spend a good twenty-minutes a day listening to relaxing music on your iPod. Either he'll be lulled into stillness or, as long as your wang isn't tone deaf, he'll pick up a few tunes and you won't need an iPod anymore.

Contrary to popular belief, marijuana does not lower your sperm count. Here is what does:

SMOKIN' FAGS: Stop smoking cigarettes, too.

BOOZIN' IT UP: Not to mention the threat of whiskey dick; however, getting drunk has the opposite effect on women. Many of my fellow moms said they got knocked up after gettin' crunk-a-lunk. Science is so mysterious.

BEING TOO FAT OR TOO SKINNY: Or maybe you just won't get any because you're too fat or too skinny.

LIVIN' AT THE GYM OR BEING A JUICE MONKEY: Too much exercise and 'roids. Score one for your Xbox-for-exercise, haven't left the couch for two days, sorry ass.

EATIN' SHIT: Not literally. Increase your vitamins A, C, and zinc, and cut the processed crap. As an added bonus, maybe you won't get scurvy again.

FREAKIN' OUT, MAN: Go smoke another one. Stress is bad.

Oh ya, and again, smoking weed doesn't fuck up your sperm, and wearing boxers instead of tightie-whities doesn't necessarily give a flagellum up to your swimmers, but you look like less of a dork wearing them.

Betcha Can't Have JUST ONE

POLYAMORY: noun; the philosophy or state of being in love or romantically involved with more than one person at the same time.

COMPERSION: noun; the feeling of joy associated with seeing a loved one love another or be loved by another; the antithesis of jealousy.

The Difference Between Polyamory, Polygamy, and Swinging

Polyamory is the practice of maintaining more than one relationship without hiding it from all those involved, whether separately (e.g., I have a husband and a boyfriend, but my boyfriend is my primary relationship) or together (e.g., a "triad," with all three partners together in one primary relationship). Some call this an open relationship.

Polygamy is being married (usually illegally) to more than one person a la weird, old school Mormons.

Swinging refers to when people have no strings attached sex with multiple partners, whether they're in a relationship or not.

One can be polyamorous, but monogamous with each participating partner; or poly and a swinger. One can be a swinger, but monogamous with their partner. One can be poly and swing with one partner, but not with the other (the other should know about it, though). Get it?

I often get asked about how to stay true to one's polyamorous lifestyle while in a loving, committed, monogamous relationship. When I figured out that I'm actually poly and didn't just have a cheating heart, I set some rules for myself:

Only enter relationships with other poly or poly-supportive people. If you're the type of person who can and will carry on more than one relationship at once, you obviously need to know that all those involved in your poly-molecule are okay with the situation. If your partner isn't poly, he/she must at least be cool with your polyamorism (i.e., you date others, but she/he just dates you).

Be honest with myself and encourage partners to do the same. If I tried to enter a monogamous relationship lying to myself that it'll work, I'd end up cheating. Conversely, if your partner claims to be okay with you seeing other people when in reality they're not, they'll be eaten alive with resentment.

Get tested for STDs on a regular basis. Also, always use protection, except maybe with your primary partner (this is why primaries are sometimes called, "fluid bonded.")

Fuck the rules. There are as many ways to have relationships as there are fools to have them. As long as everything is 100 percent open and honest for all from the get-go (inclusive of being honest with yourselves), poly or not, you'll only have to worry about the billion other things that fuck up relationships.

Q How and when should you introduce your parents to members of your polyamorous circle? My husband and I have been involved with a girl for almost a year and it's obvious to everyone around us that we're connected. How do you approach this subject? Is it okay to bring this woman to Thanksgiving inner and family barbecues? Is there a timeline for when you want to introduce someone to your family and how do we go about it? "Hey mom, this is Nicole, the girl we've been having three-ways with!" Your advice is much needed, as this is something that's coming up more often these days. *Lola*

It ain't easy being the freak of the family—trust me, there ain't many who are as freaky as I. Whether it's polyamory, swinging, homosexuality, BDSM, or transgender issues, deciding how, when and if you're going to share personal sexual issues with your kith and kin is a touchy thing. Only you truly know your relationship with your family.

What may not cause my family to blink an eye, might cause yours to disown you. How much have you shared about your alternative lifestyle with them in the past? How did that go over? When you showed up to Aunt Ida's eighty-fourth birthday wearing a collar, did you catch flak?

What about when you spilled the beans to your sister about your bicuriosity? Too chickenshit to do it? Then they're probably not ready. Sometimes we have to accept the fact that they may never be ready and an ongoing, loving relationship with them is more important to you than pushing the envelope. Sometimes we have to sacrifice for the ones we love. When everyone involved is someone you love, we need to step back and look at the big picture, in order to see the greater good. Try www.polyamorysociety.org for suggestions and support for polymolecules and polyfamilies.

Q **Does being sexually attracted to both gals and guys…I understand it makes ya bisexual, but in the long run, would—if said things didn't work out—maybe later turn you gay?** *Dan*

First off, understand that sexual orientation—contrary to right-wing conservative Christian belief—is not a choice. You can't be "turned" gay or straight. We're either homosexual, heterosexual or some combination thereof (I believe almost everyone falls into the third category). You can start out life very hetero, dally in some bisexuality a bit later, have three straight relationships in a row and end it all off with a long-running gay relationship. Are you gay? Straight?

If you're asking whether you have a greater chance of pursuing a gay relationship if you've already accepted that you're bi, compared to someone who has never thought about it at all, then yes, I suppose there is a greater chance you could end up in a strictly homosexual relationship later in life…you've just doubled your dating pool.

But I'd worry less about "turning gay" and more about following your heart. If you try to forever suppress something that is part of your being, you'll be a spiritual and psychological wreck. Love between consenting adults is never something to be avoided…nor is mind-blowingingly good sex, for that matter.

> Love between consenting adults is never something to be avoided…nor is mind-blowingingly good sex

Swing Low, Sweet Mamakind

My first real orgy experience (not just drunken, E-induced roommate groping) was at a long-since-gone-under swinger's club in Montreal, Les Libertines. It was my first time in this awesome city of style and sensuality. Accompanying me were two male friends, my then-boss, and his girlfriend at the time. There were no sexual relations between my boss and I; it was a work trip and well, let's just say, we were making the most of our travel budget and exploring all this fair city had to offer.

We initially walked into what looked like any grungy, Moe's-type bar: a mixture of flickering neon and black smokiness. We paid our cover and picked a booth where we could casually survey the scene and my comrades-in-kink could soak up some liquid courage.

Several months pregnant at the time (though not really showing), I was relying on the pre-natal-induced tsunami of hormones gushing through my body and cat-killin' curiosity to keep me from hittin' the nearest SORTIE to the street. It was one of those prohibition-damning moments where

I was left thinking, "FUCK! What I'd give to light up a joint right now…"

Someone got up to speak with the gorilla guarding (strangely enough) the back door of the place. Leaning on the bar were several young, hoochily dressed ladies softly clucking like French hens and I wondered aloud why there were so many women in a dive like this? Everyone gave each other the "she's-a-beef-eating-Prairie-girl-spooked-by-the-big-city" look and it was whispered with a piteous scowl that they were paid to be there (a.k.a "tickets") so the single guys wouldn't show up to a fish market of empty tanks. Duh!

We got a signal from the bouncer to follow him out back into the dark alley about two doors down to another door, leading into what looked like a cross between a foyer and a laundry room; shelves of white towels, a washer/dryer and large safe. The gorilla explained we could leave our personal belongings in the safe, but had to be naked in the club. We were each given a towel and warned to keep it with us at all times. The reasons for that would become apparent as the evening progressed, but hiding our glories from the world seemed reason enough at that moment.

The entire place was bathed in creepy black light; I half expected Golum to crawl down the wall. Everyone resembled amusement park haunted house spooks. Not the sexiest look. The first room was completely mirrored, with two rather sad looking futons on the floor. Two couples were in there; the girls were straddling the men, chitchatting in French as if they were waiting for the bus. There was a double shower and another shaggin' room, appropriately enough, with dark shag carpeting that resembled a mass of flattened earthworms after years of bodily fluid soakings and mashings by wiggling ass.

There was a bigger room with a good-sized hot tub in the corner. Moans of passion floated up from a set of stairs leading to some darkened abyss of smut. I dared not leave the company of my cohorts (my boss and his gal had wandered off and she could be heard wailing with pleasure nearby). Disregarding what my mother always said about public hot tubs ("They're like human soup!" and this one even more so), I plopped into the foamy boil, seeking cover for my nakedness. My friends followed. Then it seemed the whole damn room (ninety-eight percent men) followed. Suddenly, I was being probed like a Japanese schoolgirl by a multi-tentacled anime alien. Hands, fingers, tongues and cocks swarmed me, filling every orifice, prodding me to heights of joy.

After giving all participants a hearty,

"Merci!" and hitting the shower, I ran into my boss in the "common area." We both stood back, towels draped casually over our shoulders and surveyed what appeared to be a scene from Caligula. As if leaning on an imaginary water cooler:

"Hi, Mamakind."

"Hey Boss."

"Howzit going?"

"Not bad. You?"

"I'm having a great time."

"Yeah." I chortled uncomfortably, "Woo! Montreal's pretty crazy, eh?"

"I'll say. So…"

"So…I should get back."

"Oh yeah…me too. My girlfriend is getting bukkake'd in the mirror room. I should head back there, too."

"Yeah, I can hear her. I'm gonna get my own thing going in that room fulla dudes over there, so…see ya later!"

"Bye. Good luck with that."

My only legitimate complaint was the awful soft rock station lilting in the background…ick. I got gang banged to Captain and Tennille. I guess it's better than being gang banged by Captain and Tennille. Granted, one should never look a gift orgy in the fuckhole (one might get squirted in the eye). I thoroughly enjoyed myself nonetheless. The debauchery continued well into morning and into the rest of our lives, forever 'n' ever.

Cannabis 'n' Cream

As one grabs one's ankles and gets slammed in the bathroom of a sultry, Montreal after-hours party at five a.m., one waxes sentimental. I've only just moved to one of the sexiest cities on Earth and my mind keeps returning, like Pee-wee to the peep show, to what seems like a foreshadowing of French fuck fests of the future.

What was to be the final Quebec Cannabis and Hashish Cup had ended for the night, and I'd just witnessed its organizer being hauled off by the cops. I was fairly blasted and more than a little sad about the bust, but sweethotknifing Hosanna, it's motherfucking Montreal!

I hooked up with a couple of buddies (I may have a different csonnotation of "buddy" than you), one of whom was a native Montrealer who suggested going to Cream; it was Sexy Swingers Night.

My ovaries were already vibrating from the glorious sieved hash I had the pleasure of partaking in earlier. The anonymity of travel, coupled with my de rigueur exhibitionism, made me want to pin my "Hello My Name Is SLUT" button on and ride. Giddy up!

Upon arrival, I was informed of the

"sexy" dress code in effect. I undid the buttons of my blouse, revealing a black lace bra, hoping it would suffice. Never did I feel more like I just stepped off the Greyhound from CowTown.

At first glance it seemed like the usual bar: strobe lights, pounding house music, a couple of chicks that were obviously tanked, clumsily shaking their moneymakers on the little stage. There was a cage with a constant rotation of gyrating, slithering club folk. A gay bar for straight people came to mind.

Then I noticed a PYT getting fingered by her twinkie twin on the dance floor, just as some guy wearing box-

ers and a bowtie came up to me and offered to adorn my jubblies with the whipped topping he was toting. How could I have refused? I have enough room for a whole pie if need be. The place is called Cream.

Faced with such succulent pastries, my friends attempted to dutifully lick me clean (little did they know that that's an impossibility). Of course, licking turned into kissing, then biting, slapping, rubbing, sucking and squeezing. Before you could say, voulezvouscouchezavecmoi, I was getting thoroughly molested on the dance floor.

The music, lights and bodies swirled into a psychedelic-sexual mass as my nipples were rolled between two sets of teeth and what felt like more than twenty fingers probed, pinched and prodded me.

A few of them slipped under my skirt and began drumming on my clit and shallow-diving into my steaming gully. Still more fingers intertwined in my hair and pulled my head back so that my moans of ecstasy could be heard over the pulsating beat. I came so hard I thought I was either going to pass out or throw up.

An excellent cue for me to exit stage left to the nasty little girls room. After sitting on the toilet for a while with my head between my legs (I think my blood pressure was low), I heard the call of one of my buddies (apparently the "skirts only" sign is meaningless in Montreal). I directed him to my stall and invited him in.

He had just come in to check if I was all right and once his mind was eased that I was, indeed, ALL RIGHT, he fingered me once again. This time, I swear, his arm must've disappeared up to the elbow, with the amount of vigor he put into it.

I returned the favor by sucking his dick until he rapturously shot his cock smoothie down my throat.

What Was The Name of That Bar Again?

By that time I had fallen hard into my *Slut in the City* role and, like with potato chips, I ain't happy with just one. So I asked buddy A to find buddy B and send him in.

Sitting on the toilet, waiting, mindlessly stroking my ever-wet velvet valley, I contemplated what a bad girl I was and how wonderful life is and how I wished I could light up a phatty right then and there.

I was awakened from my reverie by the timid voice of my next victim, uh…I mean my other friend and I called him to my stall.

What delicious deja vu! I blew that boy like a toy trumpet. I sucked him like a vacuum. I licked him—you get the point. Through the lips and over the gums, look out tummy, here he cums! After that, we all toddled off to bed. Visions of CREAM danced in our heads. I had reached the summit on my sexual expeditions thus far.

That is, until we hooked up with a certain illustrious marijuana seed dealer the next day and now, more than half a decade later, here I am. But those tales will have to remain juicy blunts to suck down another time.

Merci, Montréal, for taking me into your heaving, corseted and tattooed bosom once more, hopefully for good. Who doesn't need a little stoned public orgy every once in a while? It's the Canadian way.

Q I have been with my girlfriend for a couple years. We now live together and enjoy almost every minute; we both work two jobs and I attend college. We love spending all the time we have together and it's great.

We both are always really stressed and get angry at each other easily, which in our case is not a terrible thing because it makes for amazing make-up sex, but we live in a single apartment with close neighbors. We make it a task to be loud and rough whenever we are getting crazy; so loud, we try to have our neighborhood hear us getting crazy.

One evening we had been drinking and smoking and we got going and we got so crazy that the police stopped by at two a.m. to tell us to keep it down. So we waited until they left and continued. The police returned an hour later and wrote me a ticket for disturbing the peace—all from us/ her screaming so loud.

When we blaze up it makes it even more intense than anything I have ever [experienced] with any woman I have been with. She was a virgin before me and I'm well experienced in the bedroom and out. I'm a master of many, many positions and styles.

Recently we've been having some intimacy issues [because] she wants a threesome with another woman, but wants me to find the woman to join our bedroom roundabout. I consistently feel that if I were to find another woman it would feel as if I were cheating or betraying her. She says that it wouldn't bother her, as long as I didn't fuck [the woman] before we had our experience with her. How [can I] find a woman for this experience and still feel I'm being faithful to the woman I love and care for? *Caleb of Nebraska*

For someone that lists breaking municipal bylaws and alienating the neighbors as a turn on, I'm quite surprised at your hesitation in facilitating a ménage à trois at the request of your lady-love, especially of the highly coveted "girl-girl-boy" sort.

Your woman is obviously feeling compersionate enough that she feels comfortable with the idea of you being with another woman. That's why she asked.

I think perhaps you, dear Caleb, are the one who doesn't have much along the compersion lines.

Maybe the idea of her being with another person—even another woman—bothers you on a level that society doesn't accept as hetro and manly: straight guys are supposed to love girls lezzing-out.

Or maybe you don't trust yourself—you might really like the other woman and break the one rule your girlfriend gave you.

It sounds like you guys have something pretty good going on. You should feel confident enough in your relationship that some NSA (no strings attached) sex shouldn't matter.

If you do, then off you go as a couple to a bar or swingers club/party and getchoself a willing participant. If you don't, then there are more pressing issues for you both to deal with than brunette or blonde.

CANNANTHROPOMORPHIZATION
The Strain Within Us All—
Which Strain Are YOU?

After years of eating, sleeping, living, and especially, breathing marijuana, I started categorizing my stoner friends by strain. A total pot-geek thing to do, for sure, but oh so fun and time consuming. What's your indica/sativa ratio?

1. You have a twenty-page report due next week. You'll most likely:
   a) Get it done in the next two days. Simple, but that's a lot of pages and you need your evenings and weekends free to take naps and watch porn.
   b) Do it the night before because although you started it right away, speed skating lessons and watching "America's Next Top Model" sidetracked you. It'll be nineteen pages—but creative!
   c) Work on it a little each weeknight, keeping your weekends free for rest and play. Twenty pages: no more, no less.

2. When it comes to food you're a:
   a) Vegan. Who can digest all that crap? Meat and dairy make you fart in yoga class.
   b) Carnivore. Your mom's from Texas and your dad's from Alberta. You can take a direct blood transfusion from an Angus cow. If it's green, it's something to smoke or has gone bad.
   c) Omnivore. A little of this, that and the other. Smorgasbords are all-day affairs.

3. You're built like:
   a) Matt Damon. Not too big, not too small. Your average Joe Shmo from Idaho.
   b) Kareem Abdul-Jabbar. Tall 'n' lean. Your size sixteen sneakers belie what really makes you a champion.
   c) Danny DeVito. Built like a boulder, your neck's just a suggestion.

4. Your dream vacation would be:
   a) Nimbin, Australia. You'll lead the Hemp Parade whilst flying high on the local outdoor.
   b) Amsterdam. A little sightseeing, a lot of coffeeshop and Red Light District browsing.
   c) Northern India. Live like the Buddha for days, blasted in a hash-hookah stupor.

5. Your main health complaint, if any,

would be:

a) Pain. Road rash from longboard-ing over the weekend, old football injuries—you're a walking commer-cial for Bengay.

b) Depression. A joint a day keeps the shrink at bay!

c) A little of this, a little of that. Hangnail? Hits from tha' bong will take care of that.

6. At the end of a major toking session you feel:

a) Ready to run a marathon, write a novel and fuck a high-end hooker

b) Ready to snuggle with a munch-ie bowl and watch "Dazed and Confused" for the nineteenth time

c) Ready to be scraped off the floor with a spatula

7. If you were reincarnated tomorrow, you'd likely be:

a) A bald eagle, soaring into the sunset

b) A pound-puppy, alternating between chasing your own tail, snoozing and humping anything that slows down

c) A heavy stone

8. Your favorite sport is (assuming officials turn a blind eye to your blood test):

a) The decathlon. Your sprinting abilities are enhanced by your shot-put skills.

b) Rugby. Nuthin' better than getting trashed 'n' stomped to a smear by a bloke named Paddy.

c) Formula One. An adrenaline junkie, you hit ninety mph to go to the Quickie Mart for smokes.

9. Your dream celebrity stoner buddy is:

a) Snoop Dogg. Smokin' indo, sippin' on gin and...tonic. What? Your name's Todd? Fo' shizzle, yo!

b) Carl Sagan. Trippin' on the cosmos, listening to acid jazz, and playin' D&D—with your mind on the physics and the physics on your mind.

c) Tommy Chong. Who? Chong? Naw, Dave's not here, man.

10. If you could squeeze some tits right now, they'd be:

a) Small and firm, like grapefruit

b) Big, soft and mind-blowing

c) Not too big, not too small, the size of Mamakind's in Montreal

KEY

1. a) 3, b) 1, c) 2
2. a) 1, b) 3, c) 2
3. a) 2, b) 1, c) 3
4. a) 1, b) 2, c) 3
5. a) 3, b) 1, c) 2
6. a) 1, b) 2, c) 3
7. a) 1, b) 2, c) 3
8. a) 2, b) 3, c) 1
9. a) 3, b) 1, c) 2
10. a) 3, b) 1, c) 2

10-13 points: HAZE

You're a day-trippin', high-flyin', late-bloomin' ganjanaut!

14-17 points: SKUNK #1

Upbeat and fun, everyone wants to hook up with you—even if you smell funny.

18-21 points: NORTHERN LIGHTS #5

Everyone loves you because you're strong, reliable and easygoing. And you make them lots of money.

22-26 points: BLUEBERRY

Your presence chills out the room and you get a lot of action. You taste so fucking good!

27-30 points: AFGHANI #1

You're a heavy hittin', couch-locked powerhouse. You matured early and fuck people up all night long.

Q There is a girl in my class at my college; I would like to find out if she smokes. Let's just say our professor is slightly elementary, with assigned seats. So what do you think would be the best way of going about asking her this without offending, on the off chance she doesn't mind if I smoke? *Wild Fire*

Are you asking because you're interested in her for scoring weed or poon (better yet, both)? Either way think, "friend," not "mark." Don't bother her during class. Maybe I saw one too many John Hughes flicks, but if you jauntily sidle up to her after class while she's walking to her next, introduce yourself in a humbled-yet-humorous manner, compliment her on her dreads and inked sleeve (there's got to be some reason you wanna ask her about weed) and ask her about how she likes the class you're both in…it's a good in (at least it worked for John Cusack). Eventually, I can guarantee, if she's a toker or dealer, the subject will come up because she'll either want to either toke with or sell to you. Maybe not on that first meeting, but if you have patience, you'll have your answer, Wild Fire. Wax on; wax off.

Q How do I tell my wife of five years, who thinks she is god's gift to joint rolling, that she sucks? Her joints always fall apart and are loose as some certain musical blonde celebs out there. She says I can't roll, but at least mine burn even and don't fall apart or lose any weed from the ends! Any help would be appreciated. Thank you.

Joint custody in trouble

It's called tact. How do you tell her anything to which you're dreading the response? First off, I'd start packing bowls until you can figure it out. Grab a potato and smoke out of that if you have to. It'll be fun! First, get

> Marijuana has helped me achieve more sex, intimacy and, yes, even love than any force save human nature.

her nice and ripped. That's the ticket. Okay, now the tricky part. Accept that she thinks your phatty construction is crappy, too. Start talking up the idea of why using glass bowls are so much better for you, and you'd save so much on papers. Or, suggest that you should invest in a reasonably priced vaporizer, because, not only is it better for you and you save on papers, it actually makes your stash stretch farther. If she still ain't buyin' it, I have two words for you: rolling machine. Don't even ask; just go out and buy one. For about five minutes, they can be a little tricky to figure out, then you'll get the swing of it. Start using that puppy for the joints you roll. At least then she'll automatically start noticing a difference between properly rolled spliffage and disintegrating shwag sticks. And maybe, just maybe, she'll notice how much herb it takes to roll with the machine and go, "Hmmm… it would be so much cheaper if I just learned to roll pinners like the machine rolls chungas, and then I can tell the ol' man to shove that rolling machine up his ass…" and you'll just smile and take it, because a well-rolled doob is almost as beautiful as the woman whom you might be lucky enough to have roll it.

Confessions of An Unkept Woman

I'm a firm believer there's someone for everyone—sometimes, several someones. From each according to their ability, to each according to their need—all that commie razzamatazz. If you're a Republican, cross-dressing, pill popping painslut, there's an equally sadistic dickweed pharmacist who shares your bra size.

What do a relationship's dynamics matter if they don't hurt anybody and everyone has their needs met—even if those dynamics are based on "shallow desires?" Is it wrong to pay for a relationship?

A while back I reviewed a "dating" site for sugar daddies, mommies and their sugar babies. I made a profile; partly for journalistic integrity, partly because I've got so much lovin' to dish out I couldn't contain it in an airplane hanger…and partly because I'm more strapped than a tweaker the day before the welly check comes.

I've problems anytime I have to create an online profile. In case you haven't noticed, I lean toward honesty usually reserved for drunkards and deathbeds. I've dabbled and blabbed about my debauchery for so long, I forget not everyone cares to know every dirty detail. The fact that I'm a writer enhances and unfortunately encourages long-winded (though exquisitely penned) autobiographies invariably involving the terms "heavy bottom," "hardcore bongslut" and "JewGut." This usually means a snitty admin will send an email stating my profile's been turned down because of "prohibited subject matter." They never say what about it was prohibitive, so we do this back-and-forth thing where I change what I think is the offensive item and it's rejected again. Eventually, I encrypt and reword every damn thing until it reads:

Description: *Fore and aft endowed, metallically enhanced, skin-doodled tall glass o' moloko*

Interests: *Smoking salmon, sucking big popsicles, getting repeatedly hit with pies and all manner of gettin' flamboozled*

It's been suggested my profile is too confusing and perhaps a tad Dali-esque. Tough titties! My personality is confusing and Dali-esque. If you can't deal with the melting clocks in my world, you just go ahead and ride that giant lobster claw outta here.

Somewhere there's a rich, num-mylicious international financier/hashmaker/sushi chef/masseuse/tattoo artist who enjoys post-deadline jaunts to Majorca and long blowjobs on the beach; who's okay with the husband, boyfriends, kids and assortment of those whom can only be described as Mamakind fetishists.

I suggested the site for a single girl-friend of mine. At first she seemed sort of offended that someone would set up a relationship as a business transaction— candy-coated prostitution. Where's the love? Where's the romance?

I said, "You're hawt, looking for company and won't date a scrub. The monorail-full of Japanese students you rent your extra bedroom to will eventually pull outta the station. That last one—Kikiko or whatever—was a total bitch hiding behind a Hello Kitty smile. And she couldn't close a door properly, as you've repeatedly pointed out."

After assessing her closet full of last-year's duds, near empty sex-toy drawer and a mani and pedi not on the calendar for another three weeks, my sister-in-crime reluctantly capitulated, put up a profile and almost immediately snagged Mr. Large.

Mr. Large is a tall, well-off, fiftyish Italian businessman (I think he said something about "waste manage-ment") who has the look and carriage of Lex Luther (minus the affinity for evil-doing). Like most fiftyish, well-off Italian businessmen, he's been happily married forever to a stunning, Botoxed trophy wife who's most likely banging the dude who details her Mercedes. Large himself has kept an assortment of side dishes over time and the couple's unspoken don't-ask-don't-tell policy has served them well over the course of their marriage.

And wouldn't you know it? My friend and Mr. Large have been seeing each other on the sly for over four years now. Sex, intimacy and yes, even love—a couple hours a week. He gets his itch scratched and she gets rid of her roommate, a new washer and dryer and her tickle trunk all filled up.

I still haven't found anyone who can simultaneously fill my bank account, bong and orifices…yet. But he (or she—I ain't picky) is out in the ether, anxiously waiting to smoke some salmon with yours truly.

Q **There is this girl. I think she likes me and I like her, so how do I ask her if she likes me or not and tell her I like her?** *Jimmy*

Believe it or not, this question wasn't passed to me on a wadded piece of gum wrapper.

Jimmy, Jimmy, Jimmy. Talk to her, man. Talk about anything—the weather, weed, music, how much grade nine bites, it doesn't matter. As long as you open the doors of dialogue. Once you start talking, it will become more and more apparent if she likes you, because if she doesn't she'll try to ditch the conversation quickly. If things stay cool, try setting up a casual second meeting; meet for coffee or something benign like that. Even better, if she's a toker like you, ask her if she wants to have a toke with you. If she doesn't partake—why are you bothering?

JUST KIDDING!

After that, it's up to you to woo. Try not to hyperventilate; make sure your fly isn't open. Good luck, soldier.

Q **I tasted tang on my boyfriend's dick. Should I dump him or just play him back?** *trichromefairy*

I assume you're talking about the poon variety of tang and astronauts aren't sucking off your boyfriend.

It's the beginning of the end if you're planning on coming home with your cooch tasting like cock. You might as well pack your relationship in, because if it's going to slip into an eye-for-an-eye (rather, poon-for-a-dick) war, neither of you will win. You'll both be bitter and driven by hurting the other, which isn't healthy for people or countries.

Ask him. If he gives you a satisfactory answer, drop it and move on. If not, dump his ass, because you'll never really trust him again and if you can't trust him, you shouldn't waste your time on him.

Q **I went to this fairly large and fancy stag (this was no beer and porn affair) and I gotta tell ya', they had the best party favors I've ever had the pleasure of partaking in. There were two humidors sitting on a table. One had some of the finest smoking Cubans**

I've had the pleasure of partaking in. Those went mighty quick.

The second though, holy shit! It was filled with about 100 perfectly machine-rolled joints separated into three sections: Sensi Star, BC God, and Jack Herer. Awesome strains to begin with, but when I picked one up I noticed a very familiar smell; they weren't any kind of flavored paper I'd ever come across. It took me a minute or two to figure it out (there was a few of us with joints to noses, the same strange smile on our faces), but then it hit me like ton of bricks: pussy! Later, the best man who threw the stag, stood up and revealed where they got these papers that I know you won't find in any head shop. He was very good friends with the bride and it was she who suggested giving each one a coochie dip, then she laid them out on a towel to dry overnight.

Let me tell you, the groom went beet red, but then he was laughing as hard as anyone. He never picked up on the smell, but if anyone would! I wonder how she managed to stay that wet that long to dip 100 joints? Crazy. *Bachelor #420*

Thanks, Bachelor #420. Those bones may just put my pussytoking to shame! From my sticking-marijuana-in-my-pussy experience, she would've had to keep rather, uh...stimulated in order to produce the amount of juice required to slather the homemade Juicy Jays. If someone's in need of such a service, feel free to email me. I got more than enough Mamakind Juice to cover a 420 rally.

Hate To Love Ya' Baby

Why is it that bad energy—more often then not—leads to such fucking awesome sex? Some of the most intense, intimate and pleasurable skronk sessions I've had were just after my man and I had a nasty blowout.

There's always this seething, groping, biting, crushing quality that smacks of primordial male aggression overcoming primordial female submission; adding to that, a woman's struggle with her own modern, assertive side being overpowered by an "old-fashioned," not-so-feminist desire to be "taken."

Oooo it's all so…bad, so it feels soooo fucking…good.

My guilt over "letting this happen" is assuaged somewhat by reminding myself that I'm in control, which is what differentiates the whole thing from rape, which is not acceptable and more about power than sex, anyway. This little transaction won't happen without my expressed consent; I am no delicate orchid, as I've pointed out before. I've also pointed out that this is the root of my submissive tendencies in general; I'm a big girl and I like to be made to feel like I'm, well…not.

But role-playing and other pre-arranged BDSM activities aren't the same as real life, spur-of-the-moment hate sex. Yeah, there—I've said it: HATE SEX. The fact is, passion knows not whether it's employed positively or negatively. Desperately wanting to penetrate someone by sinking a knife into their gullet and wanting to penetrate them by sinking a cock into their pussy aren't so far off from each other. Both are acts of passion, non-premeditated and all-consuming.

The blood that flushes your face—delivering a shot of adrenaline that sends your heart pumping and your breath heaving—will course through your veins with the same vigor if you're fucking someone or if you're fucking someone up.

Hate sex has a sense of finality to it, whether it's final or not. "This is the very last time I'm screwing/getting screwed by this asshole," is usually the thought that runs through your head as the clothes hit the floor. "I'm gonna show her/him what she/he is gonna be missing," as teeth and nails sink into

No one should tell you what you can and cannot put into your body; not the government, not your next door neighbor and not even your wife or girlfriend.

flesh. "Shit. This is fucking good fucking. Maybe I shouldn't dump her/his ass quite so quickly…" as your toes curl.

"Oh my god. What have I done? I am such a tremendous idiot," as you collapse next to each other in a sweaty, steaming pile of self-loathing.

Try not to be so hard on yourself. This is intimacy; as human beings, we crave it—need it—like the crackhead craves the rock. It may not be healthy and it may not be pretty, but it's a nat-ural and undeniable process. The only difference between love and hate is the paper-thin line that separates wanting to die in someone's arms and wanting someone to die by your hand.

All I know is that hate sex is, and always will be, just like its loving sibling. Take the time to take a toke to get a little perspective on the situation. If you're still ready to commit an act of senseless horniness, then, at the very least, you can always convince your friends and yourself that it was the pot that made you do it.

Q My man and I have a seven-month-old daughter, so our sex life isn't as great as it once was when we first got together. I need to get into the mood more, but it's really hard, considering it's like I lost the taste for sex. And I know he wants to have sex more. What can I do to be sexier or spice things up? HELP. *Rochelle*

Sometimes up to a couple of years after you have a baby, those wretched raging hormones can wreak havoc on your libido (not to mention your bladder becomes the size of a walnut). Add to that a body (hoohoo included) that is just not the same prior to breeding, the exhaustion of parenting and sleep deprivation—it's amazing we ever have sex again to make another one.

Speaking from personal experience, at seven-months-old, your baby IS old enough to spend a night with grandma or auntie—without you—and you can try the motel thing.

But if you're gonna spend the whole night being neurotic about whether the baby's okay, you're better off trying for dinner and a movie. Remind each other of how that kid ended up coming about in the first place (even if it was a broken condom in an alley behind a bar).

Mother's Gonna Help Build The Wall (To Get Some Fucking Privacy)

My boyfriend and I were sitting on a crowded bus with my five-year-old daughter, when she came out with this gem:

"Mama [yes, my kids call me Mama, too], why do you go, 'Hhhmm...uuuhhh...ooohhh,' when you're in bed with X (okay, my ex-boyfriend isn't named after a villain in a comic book; I don't need him suing my ass if I use his real name)?"

My blood ran cold while simultaneously, my cheeks turned hot and red as a baboon's ass. "Ohhhh...um...well... I um." I frantically tried to access the parenting databanks in my brain for the currently accepted age that's appropriate to talk about sex with your child, but was coming up with what to do if she's choking and the words to the Scooby-Doo theme song. X shot me a look like my girl had just shanked him with a rusty fork.

"Well, baby-boo, we're, uh…" Scooby-Doobydoo…where are you… we've got some work to do, now.

"Wrestling! You know, like, um… play fighting."

"Wrestlin'?" Oh-sweet-Joseph-with-a-hangnail, she ain't buyin' it. Shitshitshit. We can count on you, Scooby-Doo.

"We were wrestling. Soooooo… Chinatown was fun today, huh? What do you want for dinner? My, doesn't your hair look princess-like right now! Say, we should go for popsicles when we get home! Yay—popsicles!"

Kids are just too savvy nowadays. At the risk of sounding like a cardigan-and-turtleneck-wearing member of the PTA, it's that gosh-darn-diddly television. My nine-year-old came into the living room right before bed, smelling like a trailer-park man whore. Actually, my son smelled like my ex-boyfriend's feet, because he would use this free, trial-size men's body spray to make his shoes stink less. The boy had put so much on, my eyes watered as he came near.

"Um, honey? Did you put some of that cologne spray on?"

"I sure did, Mama!" He had a sheepish grin on from ear to ear.

"And did you (coughs) spray it all over your body like they do in the commercials?"

"Yup."

"May I ask, why?" I sneezed three times in quick succession.

"Because I want the ladies to chase me." I had to bite the inside of my cheek until I could taste copper, just to not laugh in the poor boy's face.

"Sooooo…what do you want them to do when they catch you?"

"Uh…I dunno. I just want them to chase me like in the commercial! It looked like fun."

Oy. It's enough to drive a Jewish mama all mishugah, I'm telling you. It's bad enough I have to deal with coitus interruptus screams of, "MAMAAAA! He's looking at meeee!!!" and silent, ghostly figures appearing in the doorway, standing there for lord-knows-how-long while I get spanked in a way in a way definitely not intended for naughty children.

Having to impart cohesive, modern, emotionally sensitive yet scientifically sound sexual wisdom to my offspring in such a way that they don't end up getting knocked-up at fourteen, knocking some fourteen-year-old up, or possibly worse: end up a thirty-six-year-old virgin.

Having to impart cohesive, modern,

emotionally sensitive yet scientifically sound sexual wisdom to you, dear readers, is not quite so, uh…pressing, shall we say. You guys are already fucked up from fucking by the time the power of the bongslut gets to ya'.

I don't mind sharing my nasty little escapades and pearls of pot-sexy wisdom with thousands of drooling stoners, but trying to not share them with the two drooling (okay, they don't really drool—that much) chilluns under my motherly watch—that's a toughie. But I do it. I manage. Hey—I don't want them blaming me when they end up on the shrink's couch in twenty years.

However, having tossed my two-cents into the gene pool, I can honestly tell you that children do temper you. It's not that I don't want to hit a different swingers club every night, a veritable wake of stems, seeds and tequila fumes following me like Janis Joplin's shadow.

But the school bus comes at 6:45 a.m., there are bologna and cheese sandwiches to make, braids to straighten and report cards to sign. Please don't get me wrong—I love my kids dearly and I'd trade them in for nary a bender, nor gangbang. But they say youth is wasted on the young. I say it's wasted on those without any young.

Q **What do you do if your man wants to have sex and you don't, even though you both haven't had it in a while?** *Tiff*

First, thank the powers that be that you have the option, whether you choose to make use of it or not. Second, why don't you want to have sex? If we're talking a week or two, that's one thing, but if it's been a really long time, then you should be questioning what happened to your sex-drive. Is it that you don't want to have sex with your man, or that you don't want to have sex at all? Illness, depression, certain medications and too much stress are some of the reasons why your libido might have flown the coop. If there's nothing to be done medically, I suggest you pick up your favorite aphrodisiac strain (I'm partial to Flo for libido-boosting, not that I have that issue very often), slip on some porn or Jonas Brothers or whatever it is that turns you on and then do what comes naturally. But the simple answer to your question is to say, "No, thank you." And that's the end of that.

Q **My girlfriend (now wife), started out being real cool with use of medical marijuana to treat migraines and insomnia. Now, when I blaze up for a headache or even a recreational** smoke, she pulls an attitude. "Do you have to smoke today? Didn't you smoke last night?" Also, I've become quite the collector of glass-on-glass pieces. She's complaining about that now, too. She claims "clutter," but I know she thinks it's immature and that weed is only for burnt-out nineteen-year-olds. I'm thirty-three and she's twenty-nine. I want her to understand that cannabis is a way of life for me—but I don't want to arouse her ire, either. She is my absolute partner and friend and I want to approach her right. Help? *MediMax*

Q Hello, Mamakind. I am writing to ask you about cannabis use when the wife hates it. Even when I make it perfectly clear there will be nothing but once-a-week, responsible use, she still goes off. Now, I see it as my American right to pursue my personal happiness, especially in a responsible manner. I've thought about just doing it behind her back when I come home from work at 5:30 a.m. on the weekends. Somehow I feel that she would prefer that, but she would never allow it if she found out. What would you recommend for my situation? Thanks. *James*

Whether you consider your cannabis use medical or recreational, someone will have a problem with it, legal or not.

It really sucks when that someone is the love of your life (I assume these ladies are the loves of your lives, otherwise, why would you put up with that shit?).

No one should tell you what you can and cannot put into your body; not the government, not your next door neighbor and not even your wife or girlfriend. However, these people frequently do just that. Solid relationships should never be about "allowing" this or "disallowing" that, nor should you have to hide anything. Honesty is the foundation of most relationships. You've got to use a little diplomacy and come to some sort of compromise.

Find out EXACTLY what her issue is. If she doesn't want the house smelling like Sparky's skid-marked ginch, take it outside. If you can't do that for whatever reason, invest in a good vaporizer that doesn't stink up the place. If she has a problem with its illegality or health factors, pick up a good book on the subject, like Lynn Zimmer and John P. Morgan's *Marijuana Myths, Marijuana Facts* and maybe it'll allay her fears.

If she doesn't like that you're spending too much money on glass, slow down on your glass purchases and only buy paraphernalia for yourself on your birthday or the holidays and be reasonable about it. No one needs six bongs, no matter how pretty they are, if you're struggling to make ends meet.

I've been an activist for the past decade and believe me, there's anti-prohibition rhetoric to match any naysayer complaint—just make sure you know what you're talking about. Saying that cannabis use is only for the immature is like saying boobs are only for babies. People are mature or immature, not substances. It's all in how you use it.

Whether you're straight, gay, bi, poly, mono, hooked-up or single, love can silently sneak up on you like ninja and hit you like Kanye West's bodyguard.

If you're immature and irresponsible in your cannabis use, she has a good point. Alcohol can be sipped out of teacups by old ladies at a quilting bee, or it can be chugged by frat boys through a funnel at a kegger.

Lastly, all you can do is try to accommodate her as much as possible, but both parties must accept the consequences of the choices you both make. If she says she'll leave you if you keep consuming cannabis, you need to decide if your lifestyle is worth your woman walking out on you, or if her disdain for your medicine is worth dumping her.

What Women Who Want Men Who Want Weed Want—and Vice Versa

I've been blessed in my, uh…exposure to the opposite sex. The fact that I'm already married opens certain doors of insight into the inner workings of Everyman's heart and mind. Because men don't have an underlying fear that I'm trying to lasso them with a ring and diaper duty, they feel comfortable pursuing our relationship in a "truer" way. They can relax and simply enjoy my presence, whether it's for a platonic friendship, single session swinging, or a long-term love-bound affair.

Unlike most of the human populous, I can differentiate between love, sex, and intimacy (it was one of the questions on the competency test for this job). I know that sex is a fun, feel-good, physical activity that really isn't that much different than, say…cross-country skiing. Some of it's an easy, swift glide; sometimes you really gotta use your brute strength to get up that hill, sweaty and incoherent in an endorphin-induced, happy stupor.

I hate snow, though, and I'd rather be naked than be caught wearing those dorky orange goggles. If I can raise my heart rate without involving Nike, Spalding, Rossingol, or random drug testing, I most certainly will.

Intimacy is a connection with someone that shoots right past our usual boundaries and defenses to affect our very core. If I were a plant (guess which one I'd be?), I'd need light, water and food to survive. Intimacy is my Über-Growth formula. Everyone needs to achieve intimacy on some level, like flashes of enlightenment to the human condition. You don't need to be fucking someone to connect with them on an intimate level—only open and willing to accept within yourself whatever beauty or beast is revealed.

Babies that are never held or cuddled, they don't grow. Not from lack of nourishment or health care. It's from a lack of intimacy. The trickiest of the three is LOVE. Anyone can make sex happen at any time (thank you Al Gore for your contribution of the Internet). You can open yourself up to intimacy and receive it right away; however, it's impossible to set oneself up for love.

Falling in love happens whether you want it or not. Whether you're straight, gay, bi, poly, mono, hooked-up or single, it can silently sneak up on you like a ninja and hit you like Kanye West's bodyguard.

Conversely, just as you can't control falling in love, you can't orchestrate falling out of it, either—neither Wild Turkey neat, nor golden honey oil vaped, can quell a heart afire. You can musically bawl along with BB King or Willie Nelson and s/he still won't come back (you pathetic loser, you) and that's why it hurts so damn much. You know all of this but no matter how much knowledge you arm yourself with there's nothing that can shield you from the bliss 'n' shit storm.

Marijuana has helped me achieve more sex, intimacy and, yes, even love than any force save human nature. Cannabinoids coursing through my veins heighten sensation; sex feels better; inhibitions are loosened and stoners are more open to gettin' it on. I've smoked hash so good that it brought me to the very brink of orgasm by the second puff.

Oxytocin is called the "cuddling hormone." Released in pulses from our reproductive organs during orgasm, it's responsible for the warm fuzzies mothers feel toward their babies and theirs alone and the desire to snuggle after a good fuck. When levels are raised we feel more trusting, which is the keystone to any intimate experience. Oxytocin is nature's intimacy potion. It turns out that pot makes the potion more potent because cannabinoids encourage oxytocin's flow.

What about love? My love of the herb has made me seek out like-minded souls. I met my husband hanging about ganja-related forums. I've experienced at least two other relationships I'd dare qualify with the L-word that were directly attributed to mutual herbaceous leanings.

So, yeah. I know all this shit and have a deeper understanding…blah, blah, blah. Where does it get me? Like draconian drug laws, it's really out of my control, right? Well, I could live consciously and honestly, holding the vision of my desires in my mind's eye —sex, intimacy, love and free weed, or a combination thereof—as I happily manifest the seemingly non-manipulatable. Or…I could bitch because I ain't got none and there ain't nothin' nobody can do about it no how—and be miserable.

Lucky for you that I'm such an enlightened gal.

Baby, Can You Spare Some Change?

Change is good for so much more than pluggin' the parking meter and weighing down your couch. Even the slightest of alterations of your relationship, from locale to switching from boy-cut to thong, will lend itself to a whole new P.O.V. (hopefully, a much clearer one).

I just finished the Alexandrian task of crisscrossing the North American continent with my boyfriend—from Montreal to Calgary to Montreal to Calgary.

It was more than an unwieldy attempt at approximating the RV-tastic journeys we might embark upon when we're white-haired and smell like Bengay.

While much of it was very pleasurable, it wasn't a pleasure trip (we're moving) so it had that slightly frenzied durm und strang that comes with vast distances, a nasty Canadian winter breathing down our necks, time and monetary restraints and an angry cat. Oh…and my bad ass got turned away at the American border. That didn't add to the love: I was really stoked to get a chance to see Fargo. Really.

You don't need to pick up and move your life 2500 miles away to benefit from

an alteration of your everyday experience. President Obama isn't the only one allowed to punctuate his every move with the promise of "change," y'know.

My suggestion to you all is to ride the wave of change that's swelled all over the land like a Sybian saddle on overdrive.

Jump on that newness bandwagon—face down and ass up. Take advantage of this metamorphosing period of history and get your groove back (if you ever had a groove in the first place and if not, go get one ya' doof). You should feel great if you had a hand in making history happen; but you'll feel even greater if you have a hand in makin' luv happen in your own personal history.